Cryptocurrency Chronicles

Unlocking the Secrets of Blockchain Technology

Simple Explanations for Complex Concepts

BY
Michael McNaught

A creatively written educational book for readers of all ages.

Interested in learning about Blockchain Technology and Cryptocurrency?

Well, this is the book for you!

Copyright

Cryptocurrency Chronicles

Understanding the Secrets of Blockchain Technology

Written By Michael McNaught

Copyright © 2023.

All Rights Reserved.

Preface

-Poem

In a world of crypto, with jargons so dense,

Investors can feel like they're on defense.

The blockchain's complexities can leave them perplexed,

And common mistakes can leave them quite vexed.

But fear not, dear reader, for there's a new guide,

That will take you on a thrilling ride.

It's called *'Cryptocurrency Chronicles*,' a true treasure,

Full of humor, memes, and insights to measure.

From blockchain technology to cryptocurrency,

This book covers it all with such clarity.

No more confusing terms or lectures that bore,

Just fun and laughter as you learn more and more.

And when it comes to growing your wealth,

This guide is worth more than good health.

It shows you how to avoid common mistakes,

And gives you the tools to make smart investment breaks.

So don't wait another moment, my friend,
For this book is the key to a successful trend.

With *'Cryptocurrency Chronicles'* by your side,
Your financial future will be your pride.

Hi there! My name is Michael McNaught, a scientist by profession, and an avid blockchain and crypto enthusiast. I enjoy learning about this amazing cutting-edge technology and sharing my knowledge with others. I got into cryptocurrency in 2021 and have progressed to building and operating mining rigs. Throughout my cryptocurrency journey, I have realized that only a very small percentage of individuals are actually knowledgeable about the fundamentals of blockchain technology and cryptocurrency.

As such, I set out to write an easily understandable and comprehensive book that gives the reader a solid understanding of the basic concepts of blockchain technology and cryptocurrency. I cover topics such as Miner, Hash, Nodes, Consensus Mechanism, Blocks and their components, crypto Wallet, Exchange, Layer 2 solutions, Memecoins, Stablecoins, Bitcoin, Ethereum, Dogecoin, Shiba Inu, and much more. I've even included a supplemental chapter, tips to keep in mind, which gives readers tips on how to make smart decisions in this ever-so-volatile industry.

Seeking a well-rounded knowledge of blockchain technology and cryptocurrency? Well, this is the book for you!

Through witty poems, and simplified and more elaborate explanations, you will gain a good understanding of the fundamentals of blockchain technology and cryptocurrency.

I do hope that you learn something new, informative and valuable. For purchasing this book, I thank you!

Table of Contents

PART I -

Cryptocurrency and Accessories

Chapter 1

Understanding Cryptocurrency

-Poem

Cryptocurrency, it's a digital world of fun,

Where coins and tokens, can make you feel like you've won.

There are meme coins, that might make you laugh,

And stable coins, that won't give you heart palpitations by the half.

Crypto wallets, they keep your coins so secure,

Like a digital bank, without any allure.

And crypto exchanges, they let you trade with ease,

Like a digital marketplace, for all your crypto needs.

And then there are the layer 2 solutions, so new,

They're like little helpers, for the blockchain to do.

They make transactions faster, like a digital flash,

And cheaper too, like a digital stash.

But sometimes understanding cryptocurrency can be quite funny,

Like trying to learn a new language, that's not very sunny.

You might get lost in the jargon, and the technical terms,

And end up feeling like, you're in a digital swirl.

And then there's the volatility, that crypto coins provide,

They can go up and down, like a digital tide.

You might get rich, or lose it all in a day,

And hope for the best, like a digital sway.

So if you ever want to understand cryptocurrency in play,

Remember, it's like a digital world of fun each day.

It's funny to think, that digital magic can be so cool,

But understanding it takes time, like a digital school!

Cryptocurrency has become an increasingly popular and mainstream topic in recent years. In this chapter, we will dive into the technical aspects of what cryptocurrency is, the difference between a coin and a token, ERC tokens, meme coins, stablecoins, wallets, exchanges, and layer 2 solutions.

-What Is Cryptocurrency?

Cryptocurrency is a digital or virtual currency that uses cryptography for security. It operates independently of a central bank and is not tied to any physical currency. Cryptocurrency transactions are recorded on a decentralized digital ledger called a blockchain, which ensures the security and immutability of the transactions.

Cryptocurrencies use decentralized systems to validate transactions and create new units of the currency. This means that the currency is not controlled by any one entity or organization, and transactions can occur between individuals without the need for intermediaries like banks or governments.

-Coins vs. Tokens

While the terms "coin" and "token" are often used interchangeably, there are some important differences between the two.

A coin is a cryptocurrency that operates on its own blockchain, it has its own native network, and functions as a currency. Examples of coins include Bitcoin, Ethereum, and Litecoin.

On the other hand, a token is a digital asset that is created and managed on top of an existing blockchain. Tokens are used to represent a variety of assets, such as digital assets, commodities, or loyalty points. Tokens can also be used to access services or products on a blockchain-based platform. Examples of tokens include ERC-20 tokens on the Ethereum blockchain and BEP-20 tokens on the Binance Smart Chain.

-ERC Tokens

ERC tokens are digital assets that are built on top of the Ethereum blockchain using the ERC (Ethereum Request for Comment) protocol. ERC tokens are essentially smart contracts that are executed on the Ethereum network and are used to represent various assets, such as cryptocurrencies, utility tokens, and security tokens.

There are several types of ERC tokens, each with its own unique characteristics and functions. Some of the most common types of ERC tokens include:

1. ERC-20: This is the most widely used token standard on the Ethereum blockchain. ERC-20 tokens are fungible, meaning that

they are interchangeable with one another and have the same value. They are often used to represent cryptocurrencies, such as Ethereum, Bitcoin, and Litecoin.

2. ERC-721: This token standard is used for non-fungible tokens (NFTs), which are unique and indivisible digital assets that represent ownership of a specific asset, such as artwork, collectibles, or in-game items.

3. ERC-1155: This token standard allows for the creation of both fungible and non-fungible tokens within a single smart contract. This makes it a popular choice for creating tokens for gaming and virtual worlds.

4. ERC-777: This token standard is designed to address some of the limitations of ERC-20 tokens, such as the inability to receive tokens that were sent to the wrong address. ERC-777 tokens can also include additional features, such as hooks that allow for automatic token redemption or token burning.

5. ERC-1400: This token standard is designed specifically for security tokens, which represent ownership in an underlying asset, such as real estate or company stock. ERC-1400 tokens have additional features that allow for compliance with securities laws and regulations.

These are just a few examples of the many types of ERC tokens that exist. Each token standard has its own unique features and uses, and new standards are constantly being developed to meet the evolving needs of the blockchain ecosystem.

-Meme Coins

Meme coins are a type of cryptocurrency that have gained popularity in recent years. They are often created as a joke or satire and are based on internet memes or cultural phenomena. Meme coins typically have no real-world utility or function, and their value is largely based on speculation and hype.

One of the most popular meme coins is Dogecoin, which was created in

2013 as a joke based on the "Doge" meme. Despite its origins as a joke, Dogecoin has become a legitimate cryptocurrency with a market capitalization in the billions of dollars.

Other examples of meme coins include Shiba Inu (SHIB) and SafeMoon (SAFEMOON), both of which have gained significant attention in the cryptocurrency community in recent months.

Cryptocurrency is a complex and rapidly evolving technology that has the potential to revolutionize the way we think about money and finance. Understanding the difference between coins and tokens, as well as the emergence of meme coins, is important for anyone looking to invest in or use cryptocurrency.

While there is still much to be learned about the potential benefits and drawbacks of cryptocurrency, it is clear that this technology is here to stay.

-Stablecoins

Stablecoins are cryptocurrencies that aim to maintain a stable value relative to another asset or benchmark, typically a fiat currency like the US dollar or Euro. The goal is to minimize the price volatility that is common in traditional cryptocurrencies like Bitcoin or Ethereum.

Stablecoins work by using a variety of mechanisms to ensure that their value remains stable. One common method is to back the stablecoin with reserves of the underlying asset, such as US dollars or gold. For example, a stablecoin may issue one unit of cryptocurrency for every US dollar in reserve, so that the value of the stablecoin is tied to the value of the US dollar.

Another approach is to use algorithmic mechanisms such as smart contracts to adjust the supply of the stablecoin based on market demand, such as by increasing or decreasing the supply of coins in circulation to maintain a stable price.

Stablecoins are useful for a variety of purposes, such as providing a stable store of value, facilitating low-cost international payments, and enabling traders to move funds quickly between different cryptocurrency exchanges without incurring currency conversion fees.

Examples of stablecoins include Tether (USDT), USD Coin (USDC), Dai (DAI), and TrueUSD (TUSD).

-Cryptocurrency Wallets

Cryptocurrency wallets are digital tools that allow individuals to store and manage their cryptocurrencies. These wallets are designed to be secure and easy to use, providing users with a safe and convenient way to access their digital assets.

There are different types of wallets available in the market, and each has its own unique features and advantages.

1. The first type of cryptocurrency wallet is a software wallet, which is a digital wallet that can be downloaded onto a computer or mobile device. One example of a software wallet is Exodus, which is a desktop wallet that supports multiple cryptocurrencies and offers a user-friendly interface. Another popular software wallet is MyEtherWallet (MEW), which is a web-based wallet that supports ERC-20 tokens on the Ethereum network.

   Metamask is also another cryptocurrency software wallet that is used as a browser extension for Google Chrome, Mozilla Firefox, and Brave browsers. It allows users to securely store, manage, and interact with their digital assets, as well as connect to decentralized applications (dDApps) on the Ethereum blockchain. Metamask is a popular choice among users who are new to the world of cryptocurrencies, as it provides a simple and user-friendly interface that is easy to navigate. It also enables users to easily switch between different Ethereum-based networks, such as the Ethereum mainnet and testnets like Ropsten and Rinkeby.

   Additionally, Metamask provides users with the ability to buy and exchange cryptocurrencies directly within the wallet, using supported fiat currencies or other cryptocurrencies. Overall, Metamask is a convenient and reliable wallet for anyone looking to securely manage and use their Ethereum-based digital assets.

2. Another type of cryptocurrency wallet is a hardware wallet, which is a physical device that stores the private keys used to access cryptocurrency. These wallets are often considered the most secure option, as they are not connected to the internet and, therefore, less susceptible to hacking.

   One popular hardware wallet is the Ledger Nano S, which supports a wide range of cryptocurrencies and provides a high level of security. Another option is the Trezor wallet, which is also highly secure and supports multiple cryptocurrencies.

3. A third type of cryptocurrency wallet is a paper wallet, which is a physical piece of paper that contains the private keys needed to access cryptocurrency. Paper wallets are often used as a backup option or for long-term storage, as they are not susceptible to cyber attacks or hacking. However, they are vulnerable to physical damage or loss. One example of a paper wallet is Bitaddress.org, which is a free and open-source tool for generating paper wallets.

4. There are also mobile wallets, which are similar to software wallets but are designed for use on mobile devices. These wallets are convenient for individuals who need to access their cryptocurrencies on the go. One popular mobile wallet is the Trust Wallet, which supports a wide range of cryptocurrencies and offers a user-friendly interface. Another option is the Coinbase Wallet, which is integrated with the Coinbase exchange and allows for easy trading and storage of cryptocurrencies.

-Cryptocurrency Exchange

Cryptocurrency exchanges are platforms that allow individuals to buy, sell, and trade cryptocurrencies using fiat currencies or other cryptocurrencies. These exchanges provide a convenient and accessible way for users to access the cryptocurrency market and exchange their digital assets with other users.

There are different types of cryptocurrency exchanges, each with its own unique features and advantages.

1. The first type of cryptocurrency exchange is a centralized exchange, which is owned and operated by a single entity or company. Centralized exchanges are the most common type of exchange, and they provide a high level of liquidity and ease of use. One popular centralized exchange is Binance, which is based in Malta and is one of the largest exchanges in terms of trading volume. Another example is Coinbase, which is based in the United States and is known for its user-friendly interface and wide range of supported cryptocurrencies.

2. A second type of cryptocurrency exchange is a decentralized exchange (DEX), which operates on a decentralized network and allows users to trade cryptocurrencies without the need for a central authority or intermediary. DEXs provide users with a high degree of privacy and security, as they do not require users to disclose their personal information or store their assets on the exchange. One popular DEX is Uniswap, which is built on the Ethereum blockchain and allows users to trade ERC-20 tokens without the need for an intermediary.

3. Another type of cryptocurrency exchange is a peer-to-peer (P2P) exchange, which allows users to trade cryptocurrencies directly with one another without the need for a central authority or intermediary. P2P exchanges provide users with a high degree of privacy and security, as they allow users to trade with one another without disclosing their personal information. One popular P2P exchange is LocalBitcoins, which allows users to buy and sell Bitcoin using a wide range of payment methods.

4. Finally, there are also derivative exchanges, which allow users to trade cryptocurrency futures, options, and other derivative products. Derivative exchanges provide users with the ability to profit from changes in the cryptocurrency market without actually owning the underlying asset. One popular derivative

exchange is BitMEX, which is based in the Seychelles and allows users to trade Bitcoin and other cryptocurrencies using leveraged contracts.

-Layer 2 Solution

A layer 2 solution is a scalability technique that seeks to address the limitations of the base layer of a blockchain network. Layer 2 solutions aim to improve the throughput and efficiency of blockchain networks by moving some of the computation and storage off the main blockchain and onto secondary layers.

The base layer of a blockchain network, such as Bitcoin or Ethereum, is responsible for processing all transactions and storing all data on the blockchain. This can lead to scalability issues, as the base layer has a limited capacity for processing transactions, and each transaction requires significant computational resources and time to process.

Layer 2 solutions build on top of the base layer and aim to increase the network's transaction processing capacity by offloading some of the computation and storage onto secondary layers. These secondary layers can include state channels, sidechains, or off-chain protocols that operate independently of the base layer but still maintain a connection to it.

By moving some of the processing and storage off the base layer, layer 2 solutions can improve the network's speed, throughput, and efficiency while maintaining its security and decentralization. Layer 2 solutions can also reduce transaction fees and increase the number of transactions that can be processed per second, making the network more accessible and user-friendly.

Some examples of layer 2 solutions include Lightning Network for Bitcoin, Polygon (MATIC) for Ethereum, and Plasma for Ethereum. These layer 2 solutions have been designed to address the scalability issues of their respective base layers and provide faster, cheaper, and more efficient transactions for users.

In this chapter, we explored the fundamentals of cryptocurrency, beginning with an explanation of what cryptocurrency is and how it differs from traditional fiat currency. We also discussed the difference between coins and tokens, the different types of tokens, and the role they play in the cryptocurrency ecosystem. Meme coins and stablecoins were introduced, with a focus on their unique characteristics and use cases. We then delved into wallets, exchanges, and layer 2 solutions, which are all essential components of the cryptocurrency ecosystem.

PART II -

Blockchain Technology

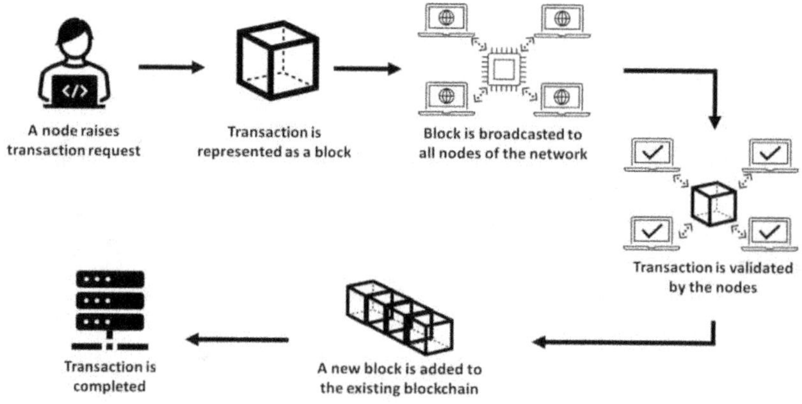

The flow of transactions in a blockchain

Image from Raja Santhi A, et al. [1]

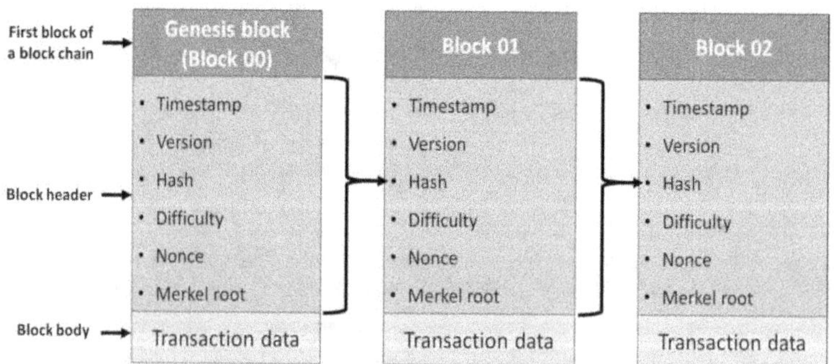

A visual description of a Block and its components

Image from Raja Santhi A, et al. [1]

Chapter 1

Understanding Blockchain Technology

-Poem

Oh, blockchain technology, so complex and deep,

It can make even the smartest among us weep.

The blocks, the chains, the nodes, and more,

It's enough to make our brains feel sore.

To understand this tech without delay, there is a way.

It's called *'Cryptocurrency Chronicles,'* and it's a real treat.

Full of humor and insight that can't be beat.

From mining to cryptography, it covers it all,

In a way that won't make your brain hit a wall.

No more confusion or feelings of dread,

Just easy-to-understand concepts instead.

And once you've got the hang of this new tech,

You'll feel like a pro, with skills that can't be wrecked.

You'll know how to invest and make smart moves,

And blockchain technology will no longer be a groove.

So don't be afraid of this new frontier,

For with *'Cryptocurrency Chronicles,'* you'll have no fear.

Just read, learn, and laugh with glee,

And soon, blockchain technology will be your cup of tea!

-The Simplified Explanation

Blockchain technology is the gift that keeps on giving. It's like a fancy digital diary that everyone can see, but no one can edit, except for those pesky hackers, of course! Think of it as a game of Jenga, where each block represents a transaction, and every time a new block is added, the whole tower gets taller and more stable, well, hopefully.

It's like a never-ending game of Tetris, but instead of clearing rows, you're securing your financial future. And, just like a game of Tetris, the more blocks you add, the harder it gets to keep everything organized and the more stressed out you become.

So, blockchain technology is like a game of digital Jenga-Tetris that could either make you a millionaire or leave you crying in the corner. Fun, right?

-The Full Story

Blockchain technology has emerged as a transformative innovation that promises to revolutionize the way we store, transfer, and verify data. It is a decentralized and distributed ledger technology that allows multiple parties to store, verify, and transfer data in a secure and transparent way.

In this section, we will explore the technical aspects of blockchain technology, including its underlying principles, components, and features.

-Principles of Blockchain Technology

At its core, blockchain technology is based on four key principles:

1. Decentralization: Blockchain is a decentralized technology that is not owned or controlled by any single entity. It operates on a network of interconnected computers, called nodes, that work together to maintain the integrity of the network.

2. Transparency: All transactions on the blockchain are transparent and visible to all participants in the network. This creates a level of trust and accountability that is not possible with traditional centralized systems.

3. Immutability: Once a transaction is recorded on the blockchain, it cannot be altered or deleted. This ensures that the data stored on the blockchain is tamper-proof and cannot be manipulated.

4. Security: Blockchain technology uses cryptographic algorithms to ensure the security and privacy of data stored on the network. This makes it virtually impossible for unauthorized users to access or manipulate data on the blockchain.

-Components of Blockchain Technology

Blockchain technology is made up of three main components:

1. Blocks: A block is a collection of data that is stored on the blockchain. Each block contains a unique digital signature, called a hash, that identifies the block and ensures its integrity.

2. Nodes: Nodes are the individual computers that make up the blockchain network. They work together to validate transactions, create new blocks, and maintain the integrity of the network.

3. Consensus Mechanisms: Consensus mechanisms are the protocols that ensure that all nodes on the network agree on the state of the blockchain. These mechanisms vary depending on the

blockchain platform, but they generally involve a process of validation and verification to ensure that all transactions are accurate and legitimate.

-Features of Blockchain Technology

Blockchain technology has several key features that make it unique and powerful. These include:

1. Distributed Ledger: The blockchain is a distributed ledger that is stored on multiple nodes across the network. This makes it difficult for any single entity to control or manipulate the data stored on the blockchain.

2. Smart Contracts: Smart contracts are self-executing contracts that are stored on the blockchain. They automatically execute when certain conditions are met, which eliminates the need for intermediaries or third parties.

3. Cryptography: Blockchain technology uses cryptographic algorithms to ensure the security and privacy of data stored on the network. This makes it virtually impossible for unauthorized users to access or manipulate data on the blockchain.

4. Tokenization: Many blockchain platforms use tokens, or cryptocurrencies, to facilitate transactions on the network. These tokens can be used to represent assets, such as real estate or stocks, and can be traded or exchanged on the blockchain.

In conclusion, blockchain technology is a powerful and transformative innovation that promises to revolutionize the way we store, transfer, and verify data. Its underlying principles of decentralization, transparency, immutability, and security, combined with its components of blocks, nodes, and consensus mechanisms, make it a unique and powerful technology with many potential applications in a wide range of industries.

Chapter 2

Types of Blockchain

-Poem

There are many types of blockchain, that's for sure,

But don't worry, my friend, it's not a bore.

From public to private, they each have their perks,

And with this funny poem, you'll understand how it works.

First up is public, the most well-known type,

It's decentralized and open, like a big ripe hype.

Anyone can join, without any fuss,

And all the transactions are transparent, without any hush.

Next up is private, which is more exclusive,

It's controlled by a group, which can be quite elusive.

It's perfect for businesses that want to keep things in-house,

And only those with permission can enter, just like a mouse.

Then there's consortium, a hybrid of sorts,

It's controlled by multiple groups, with all their cohorts.

It's great for partnerships that want to share data,

And with this blockchain type, there's no need to be a data-hater.

Last but not least, there's hybrid, the ultimate mix,

It's a blend of public and private, like fancy tricks.

It combines the best of both worlds, in a perfect mix,

And with this blockchain type, there's nothing you'll miss.

So there you have it, my friend, the types of blockchain in a rhyme,

Hopefully, you've learned something new and had a good time.

Just remember to choose the one that suits your needs,

And with this knowledge, you'll surely succeed!

-The Simplified Explanation

Imagine you have a notebook and you want to keep track of your expenses. You can write down each expense on a new page and keep the pages in order to see how much you spent over time. This is like a public blockchain, where everyone can see all the transactions that have happened and their order.

Now imagine you have a diary where you record your thoughts and feelings. You can write down anything you want, but you're the only one who can read it. This is like a private blockchain, where only certain people have access to the information stored within it.

There are also hybrid blockchains, which are like a combination of the public and private notebooks. They allow for both public and private transactions, so some information is visible to everyone, while other information is kept private. Think of it like having a notebook where some pages are available for everyone to read, while others are locked and only certain people can access them.

-The Full Story

Blockchain technology has evolved significantly since the first implementation of Bitcoin in 2009. Today, there are several types of blockchains that are tailored to different use cases and industries. In this section, we will explore the different types of blockchains, including public, private, and hybrid blockchains, and examine their unique features and use cases.

-Public Blockchain

A public blockchain, also known as a permissionless blockchain, is a decentralized network that allows anyone to participate in the network, verify transactions, and add new blocks to the chain. A public blockchain is open and transparent, and anyone can access the data stored on the blockchain. Bitcoin, Ethereum, and Litecoin are examples of public blockchains.

One of the key advantages of a public blockchain is its decentralized nature, which makes it difficult for any single entity to control or manipulate the data stored on the blockchain. However, this also makes the public blockchain less secure, as it is vulnerable to 51% attacks, where a single entity controls the majority of the computing power on the network.

-Private Blockchain

A private blockchain, also known as a permissioned blockchain, is a closed network that is restricted to a group of authorized participants. A private blockchain is more secure than a public blockchain, as only authorized participants can access the data stored on the network. This makes it well-suited for applications that require high levels of privacy and security, such as financial services, healthcare, and government.

Unlike a public blockchain, a private blockchain is controlled by a central authority, which makes it less decentralized. However, this also makes it more scalable and efficient, as the network can be optimized for the specific use case and industry.

-Hybrid Blockchain

Hybrid A hybrid blockchain is a combination of public and private blockchains. It allows organizations to leverage the benefits of both public and private blockchains, by creating a private blockchain that is connected to a public blockchain network. This allows authorized participants to access the private blockchain network, while also benefiting from the decentralized nature and transparency of the public blockchain network.

The Hybrid blockchain is well-suited for applications that require high levels of security and privacy, while also requiring transparency and decentralization. Supply chain management, asset tracking, and healthcare are examples of industries that could benefit from hybrid blockchains.

-Consortium Blockchain

A consortium blockchain is a type of private blockchain that is owned and operated by a consortium of organizations. It is similar to a private blockchain, but with multiple organizations serving as nodes on the network. This allows organizations to share data and collaborate on shared applications, while also maintaining high levels of security and privacy.

The consortium blockchain is well-suited for applications that require collaboration between multiple organizations, such as supply chain management, logistics, and finance.

In conclusion, there are several types of blockchain, each with its unique features and use cases. A public blockchain is open and transparent, but less secure, while a private blockchain is closed and secure, but less decentralized. Hybrid blockchains and consortium blockchains offer a combination of both, making them well-suited for applications that require a balance of security, privacy, and transparency.

Chapter 3

Consensus Mechanisms

-Poem

When it comes to consensus mechanisms, there are quite a few,

But don't worry, my friend, we'll make it easy for you.

From Proof of Work to Proof of Stake, they all have their charms,

And with this funny poem, you'll be the master of the blockchain farm.

First up is Proof of Work, the original and true,

It's the one that started it all, it's been tried and true.

Miners race to solve complex math equations,

And the winner gets the prize, with no hesitations.

Next up is Proof of Stake, a newer technique,

It's all about holding tokens, no need to be a geek.

The more you have, the more you can validate,

And with this consensus mechanism, there's no need to debate.

Then there's delegated Proof of Stake, a more democratic way,

Validators are voted in, to keep the network okay.

They're trusted to make the right decisions,

And with this consensus mechanism, there's no divisions.

Last but not least, there's practical Byzantine fault tolerance,

It's a mouthful, I know, but it's worth the utterance.

It's all about nodes agreeing on a transaction,

And with this consensus mechanism, there's no need for any traction.

So there you have it, my friend, the consensus mechanisms in a verse,

Hopefully, you've learned something new and had a good time, no curse.

Just remember to choose the one that suits your blockchain needs,

And with this knowledge, you'll surely succeed!

-The Simplified Explanation

Imagine you and your friends are trying to decide what pizza toppings to order. There are different options, and everyone has their preferences. One way to reach a consensus is for everyone to vote on their favorite toppings, and then the topping with the most votes is chosen. This is similar to how a blockchain consensus mechanism works.

In a blockchain network, different computers called nodes are trying to agree on the same information, such as which transactions are valid and in what order they should be recorded. To do this, they use a consensus mechanism that allows them to reach an agreement without a central authority.

One common consensus mechanism is called Proof of Work, which works like a competition where nodes solve complex mathematical problems to validate transactions and earn rewards. Other consensus mechanisms, like Proof of Stake, use a different approach where nodes are selected based on the amount of cryptocurrency they hold as collateral.

Ultimately, the goal of a consensus mechanism is to ensure that everyone in the network agrees on the same information without the need for a central authority or intermediary.

-The Full Story

Consensus mechanisms are an essential part of any blockchain network, as they ensure that all nodes on the network agree on the current state of the ledger. In this section, we will discuss what consensus mechanisms are, why they are necessary, and some of the most popular types of consensus mechanisms used in blockchain networks.

-What Is a Consensus Mechanism?

A consensus mechanism is a set of rules and protocols that govern how nodes on a blockchain network reach agreement on the current state of the ledger. This is necessary because blockchain networks are decentralized, which means that there is no central authority to verify transactions and maintain the ledger.

Instead, nodes on the network work together to validate transactions and add them to the blockchain. To ensure that all nodes agree on the current state of the blockchain, a consensus mechanism is used to coordinate the validation process.

-Why Are Consensus Mechanisms Necessary?

Consensus mechanisms are necessary in blockchain networks for several reasons:

1. Decentralization: Blockchain networks are decentralized, which means that there is no central authority to verify transactions and maintain the ledger. Consensus mechanisms enable nodes on the network to work together to validate transactions and add them to the blockchain.

2. Security: Consensus mechanisms ensure that transactions are validated by a majority of nodes on the network. This makes it difficult for malicious actors to manipulate the ledger or launch attacks on the network.

3. Trust: Consensus mechanisms create a level of trust among nodes on the network, as all nodes agree on the current state of the ledger. This makes it possible for nodes to transact with each other without the need for intermediaries.

-Types of Consensus Mechanisms

There are several types of consensus mechanisms used in blockchain networks, including:

1. Proof of Work (PoW): In PoW, nodes on the network compete to solve a complex mathematical problem, and the first node to solve the problem gets to add the next block to the blockchain.

2. Proof of Stake (PoS): In PoS, nodes on the network stake a certain amount of their cryptocurrency holdings to become validators. Validators are then chosen at random to add new blocks to the blockchain.

3. Delegated Proof of Stake (DPoS): In DPoS, token holders vote for a set of delegates who are responsible for validating transactions and adding new blocks to the blockchain.

4. Byzantine Fault Tolerance (BFT): In BFT, a set of nodes is responsible for validating transactions and adding them to the blockchain. To achieve consensus, a certain number of validators must agree on the current state of the blockchain.

In conclusion, consensus mechanisms are an essential part of any blockchain network, as they ensure that all nodes on the network agree on the current state of the ledger. There are several types of consensus mechanisms used in blockchain networks, each with its own advantages and disadvantages. The choice of consensus mechanism depends on the specific requirements of the network.

Chapter 4

Blockchain Blocks

-Poem

In the world of blockchain, there's a Block so dear,

Full of data, hashes, and blocks of cheer.

It's got a header, with all the goods,

And a Merkle tree root, that's misunderstood.

The nonce is there, with a number so fine,

It's like a lottery ticket, of digital design.

The transaction data is quite a sight,

It's verified and true, with all its might.

The block height is tall, like a tower so grand,

It's a measure of the chain, from the very first strand.

And the hash, oh the hash, it's the king of the pack,
It links all the blocks, with a cryptographic knack.

But what happens when the Block gets tired,
And all its data starts to get wired?

It takes a break, and kicks up its feet,
And enjoys a cup of tea, oh so sweet.

But then it remembers its digital fate,
And gets back to work, before it's too late.

It double-checks its hash, and its Merkle tree,
And makes sure its nonce is as lucky as can be.

And soon enough, it's back in the game,
Adding blocks to the chain, with a sense of fame.

The Block knows that it's special, in every way,
A vital part of the blockchain, come what may.

It's got a job to do, and it's doing it right,
Keeping the blockchain safe, day and night.

-The Simple Explanation

Imagine you're building a tower out of LEGO bricks. Each time you add a new section to the tower, you create a new layer of bricks that are connected to the previous layer. This is similar to how a blockchain block works.

In a blockchain network, a block is a group of transactions that are verified and added to the chain. It contains several components, including a header, a hash, and the actual transactions. The header contains important information about the block, such as the timestamp, the previous block's hash, and the block's own hash.

The hash is a unique code that is generated from the information in the block and ensures the block cannot be altered without changing the hash. The transactions themselves are records of information, such as the amount and sender of a cryptocurrency transfer. Once a block is added to the chain, it cannot be changed without invalidating the entire chain, which makes it a secure way to record and verify transactions.

-The Full Story

A blockchain is a digital ledger that consists of a series of blocks that are linked together in chronological order. Each block contains a set of transactions, and once a block is added to the blockchain, it cannot be altered or deleted. In this section, we will discuss the different components of a blockchain block and how they work together to ensure the security and immutability of the blockchain.

-Block Components

1. Block Header: The block header contains important information about the block, including its version number, timestamp, and a reference to the previous block in the blockchain.

2. Merkle Tree Root: The Merkle tree root is a hash of all the transactions contained in the block. It is used to ensure that the transactions in the block cannot be altered without also altering the Merkle tree root.

3. Nonce: The nonce is a random number that is added to the block header during the mining process. Miners change the nonce repeatedly until the block header meets a certain difficulty level, which is determined by the blockchain protocol.

4. Transactions: Transactions are the data that is stored in the

blockchain. Each transaction contains information about the sender, the recipient, and the amount of cryptocurrency being transferred.

5. Block Height: The block height is the number assigned to a block in the blockchain. It represents the position of the block in the blockchain relative to other blocks.

6. Hash: The hash is a digital fingerprint of the block. It is calculated by running the block header and all of its transactions through a cryptographic hash function. The resulting hash is unique to the block and is used to verify the integrity of the block.

-Block Validation

To validate a block, nodes on the network must first verify that the block header contains a valid reference to the previous block in the blockchain. They then validate each transaction in the block by verifying the digital signatures and ensuring that the sender has sufficient funds to make the transfer.

Once all transactions have been validated, the nodes on the network compete to solve the cryptographic puzzle contained in the nonce. The first node to solve the puzzle and add the block to the blockchain receives a reward in the form of cryptocurrency.

In conclusion, blockchain blocks consist of several components, including the block header, Merkle tree root, nonce, transactions, block height, and hash. These components work together to ensure the security and immutability of the blockchain. Nodes on the network must validate each block before it can be added to the blockchain, ensuring that the blockchain remains secure and trustworthy.

Chapter 5

Hash Functions

-Poem

In the land of crypto, there's a function so neat,

That makes the blockchain secure, with a digital beat.

It's called the hash function, and it's quite the charm,

Turning data into hashes, like a digital farm.

It takes in a block, with transactions so true,

And transforms it into a hash, like a witch's brew.

The hash is unique, like a unicorn's horn,

And helps to keep the blockchain safe, from dusk till dawn.

It might take a number, and turn it upside down,

Or make a hash that looks like a clown.

And then there are the miners, with their machines so strong,

They solve the puzzles, and find the nonce, all day long.

They use the hash function, to make the blockchain right,

And keep the network safe, through the day and night.

So if you ever see a hash function in play,

Remember, it's making the blockchain secure, in every way.

-The Simplified Explanation

Imagine you have a secret recipe for a delicious cake. You want to share the recipe with your friend, but you don't want anyone else to know the exact ingredients. One way to do this is to write down a code that represents the recipe, like a series of numbers and letters. This code is like a blockchain hash.

In a blockchain network, a hash is a unique code that is generated from the information in a block. It's like a fingerprint for the block, because if any information in the block changes, the hash will also change.

The hash is created using a complex mathematical function that takes in all the data in the block and outputs a fixed-length code. This code is then used to link the block to the previous block in the chain, creating a secure and tamper-proof record of all transactions.

The components of a hash include the data from the block and a random value called a nonce, which is used to make the hash unique. By checking the hash of a block, anyone can verify that the data in the block has not been tampered with.

-The Full Story

In the world of blockchain, hash functions play a critical role in ensuring the integrity and security of data stored on the blockchain. In this section, we will explore what hash functions are, how they work, and their importance in the context of blockchain technology.

-What Is a Hash Function?

A hash function is a mathematical function that takes an input (also known as the "message" or "data") and produces a fixed-size output, which is the hash value. In the context of blockchain, the input is typically a block of transaction data, and the hash value is used to uniquely identify and secure that block.

-Hash functions have several important properties, including:

1. Deterministic: Given the same input, the hash function will always produce the same output.

2. One-way: It is computationally infeasible to reverse-engineer the input from the output (i.e., it is very difficult to determine the input from the hash value).

3. Collision-resistant: It is very difficult to find two different inputs that produce the same output.

-How Does a Hash Function Work in the Context of Blockchain?

In the context of blockchain, a hash function is used to secure each block of transaction data. Each block contains a unique "hash pointer" that points to the previous block's hash value. This creates a chain of blocks, with each block containing the hash value of the previous block, hence the name "blockchain."

When a new block is added to the blockchain, its hash value is calculated by running the block's transaction data through a hash function. The resulting hash value is then added to the new block, along with the hash value of the previous block. This creates a secure chain of blocks, with each block's hash value depending on the hash value of the previous block.

-The Importance of Hash Functions in Blockchain

Hash functions play a critical role in ensuring the security and integrity of data stored on the blockchain. Because hash functions are one-way and collision-resistant, they make it nearly impossible to tamper with data stored on the blockchain without being detected. In other words, once a block has been added to the blockchain, it is nearly impossible to change or remove that block without breaking the chain and rendering the entire blockchain invalid.

In conclusion, hash functions are a crucial component of blockchain technology. They ensure the security and integrity of data stored on the blockchain by creating a unique, tamper-proof hash value for each block of transaction data. The use of hash functions makes it nearly impossible to tamper with data stored on the blockchain, making it a reliable and secure way to store and transfer data.

Chapter 6

Blockchain Nodes

-Poem

In the world of blockchain, there's a node so grand,
With data stored securely, all across the land.

It's like a little computer, with a job to do,
Keeping the blockchain safe, for me and for you.

The node's a part of the network, with a role to play,
Sharing data with other nodes, day after day.

It's like a busy bee, always on the move,
Collecting blocks and transactions, with a groove.

It might get confused, and send data to the wrong place,
Or get overloaded, and slow down the pace.

And then there are the miners, with their machines so strong,

They use the nodes to broadcast, and verify all day long.

They rely on the nodes, to make the blockchain right,

And keep the network safe, through the day and night.

So if you ever see a blockchain node in action,

Remember, it's working hard, with a passion.

-The Simplified Explanation

A blockchain node is like a computer that's connected to a network of other computers that are all working together to store and verify transactions on a blockchain. Imagine a group of friends sitting around a table playing a game of cards. Each friend has their own deck of cards and is responsible for shuffling and dealing the cards.

In a similar way, each node on a blockchain network has a copy of the entire blockchain and is responsible for verifying new transactions and adding them to the chain. When someone makes a transaction on a blockchain, like buying a new item with cryptocurrency, it gets broadcast to all the nodes on the network. Each node then checks to make sure the transaction is valid, using complex algorithms and cryptography, before adding it to the chain.

Once the transaction is added, it becomes part of the permanent record and can't be changed or erased. This makes blockchain technology very secure and transparent, as all the transactions are visible to anyone on the network.

-The Full Story

A blockchain node is a critical component of the blockchain network. In this section, we will explore what a blockchain node is, its functions, and the different types of nodes.

-What Is a Blockchain Node?

A blockchain node is a computer or device connected to a blockchain network. It is responsible for storing, validating, and relaying transactions and blocks to other nodes on the network. Each node on the blockchain network maintains a copy of the blockchain ledger, allowing it to verify transactions and blocks independently.

-Functions of a Blockchain Node

A blockchain node performs several essential functions, including:

1. Transaction Verification: The node verifies each transaction on the network to ensure its validity.

2. Block Validation: The node validates each block added to the blockchain to ensure it meets the network's consensus rules.

3. Network Communication: The node communicates with other nodes on the network to exchange transactions and block data.

4. Consensus Participation: The node participates in the consensus mechanism of the network, helping to maintain the network's security and integrity.

-Types of Blockchain Nodes

There are several types of blockchain nodes, each with a different function and level of participation in the network. These include:

1. Full Nodes: Full nodes maintain a complete copy of the blockchain ledger, allowing them to independently verify transactions and blocks. They participate in the consensus mechanism of the network and are crucial for maintaining the network's security.

2. Light Nodes: Light nodes store only a fraction of the blockchain data, relying on other nodes to provide the missing information. They are less resource-intensive than full nodes but offer less security.

3. Masternodes: Masternodes are nodes that perform additional functions beyond the standard node operations. These functions

may include voting on network proposals or facilitating instant transactions.

4. Mining Nodes: Mining nodes are specialized nodes that participate in the network's Proof of Work consensus mechanism by solving complex mathematical problems to validate transactions and add new blocks to the blockchain.

In conclusion, a blockchain node is a critical component of the blockchain network, responsible for maintaining the network's security and integrity. Nodes perform several essential functions, including transaction verification, block validation, network communication, and consensus participation. There are several types of nodes, each with a different function and level of participation in the network. Understanding the role of blockchain nodes is essential for understanding the blockchain network's overall operation and security.

Chapter 7

Blockchain Miners

-Poem

In the land of crypto, there's a miner so bold,
With a computer so powerful, it never gets old.

It's like a digital prospector, searching for gold,
Digging through the blockchain, with a story untold.

The miner's job is to solve a puzzle so hard,
To find the nonce, like a lucky card.

It takes lots of work, and electricity too,
But the rewards are worth it, that's for sure true.

The miner's like a hero, with a mission to achieve,
To add new blocks to the chain, and make them believe.

They use their machines, with GPUs or ASICs so strong,

And compete with each other, all day long.

They might get stuck, with a puzzle too tough,

Or make a mistake, and end up with a bluff.

And then there are the fees, that come with each transaction,

The miners collect them, like a digital attraction.

They rely on these fees to make a profit, it's true,

And keep the blockchain running, like a dream come due.

So if you ever see a blockchain miner at play,

Remember, they're working hard, every day.

-The Simplified Explanation

A blockchain miner is like a gold digger searching for gold nuggets in a river. In a blockchain network, miners use powerful computers to solve complex mathematical problems in order to validate new transactions on the network. Just like a gold digger who spends a lot of time and energy sifting through rocks and gravel to find a valuable nugget, miners compete against each other to solve these mathematical problems and add new blocks to the blockchain.

When a miner successfully solves a mathematical problem, they add a new block to the chain and receive a reward in the form of cryptocurrency, much like a gold digger who finds a valuable nugget gets to keep it. This process is called mining, and it helps to keep the blockchain network secure and decentralized, as each miner competes fairly to validate new transactions and add them to the chain. The more miners there are on a network, the more secure it becomes, as it becomes increasingly difficult for any one miner or group of miners to manipulate the blockchain.

-The Full Story

In this section, we will explore what a blockchain miner is, how they contribute to the blockchain network, and the different types of mining algorithms used in the blockchain ecosystem.

-What Is a Blockchain Miner?

A blockchain miner is a participant in the blockchain network who is responsible for validating transactions and adding new blocks to the blockchain. Miners use specialized software and hardware to solve complex mathematical problems and verify the validity of transactions.

Once a miner has validated a block, it is added to the blockchain, and the miner receives a reward in the form of cryptocurrency.

-Mining Process

The mining process involves several steps, including:

1. Transaction Verification: Miners verify transactions on the network, ensuring that they are valid and meet the network's consensus rules.

2. Block Creation: Once a miner has validated a set of transactions, they combine them into a block and add a unique cryptographic signature to the block.

3. Solving the Hash Puzzle: Miners use specialized hardware and software to solve a complex mathematical puzzle known as a hash function. The first miner to solve the puzzle and add the block to the blockchain receives a reward.

4. Block Validation: Once a miner has solved the hash puzzle, other nodes on the network validate the block to ensure that it meets the network's consensus rules.

-Types of Mining Algorithms

There are several types of mining algorithms used in the blockchain ecosystem, each with different characteristics and requirements. These include:

1. Proof of Work (PoW): PoW is the most widely used mining algorithm in the blockchain ecosystem. It requires miners to solve a complex mathematical problem, which requires significant computational power and energy consumption.

2. Proof of Stake (PoS): PoS is an alternative to PoW that requires miners to hold a certain amount of cryptocurrency as a stake in the network. The likelihood of a miner being selected to add a block to the blockchain is proportional to their stake in the network.

3. Proof of Capacity (PoC): PoC requires miners to use storage space on their hard drives to store a large number of precomputed hash values. This algorithm is less energy-intensive than PoW and PoS.

4. Proof of Authority (PoA): PoA is a consensus mechanism used in private blockchain networks. It requires a select group of validators to verify transactions and add blocks to the blockchain.

In conclusion, a blockchain miner is a participant in the blockchain network responsible for validating transactions and adding new blocks to the blockchain. The mining process involves several steps, including transaction verification, block creation, solving the hash puzzle, and block validation.

There are several types of mining algorithms used in the blockchain ecosystem, each with different characteristics and requirements. Understanding the role of blockchain miners and the different mining algorithms is crucial for understanding the overall operation and security of the blockchain network.

Chapter 8

Proof of Work

-Poem

In the world of blockchain, there's a proof so grand,
That keeps the network secure, like a digital band.

It's called Proof of Work, and it's quite the feat,
Turning computer power, into a competition so sweet.

The miners compete, with their machines so strong,
Solving puzzles all day, like a never-ending song.

They use their GPUs and ASICs, to find the nonce so rare,
And add new blocks to the chain, without a care.

The miners might get tired, and take a nap,
Or get distracted, by a digital app.

And then there's the energy, that Proof of Work demands,

It takes lots of electricity, like a digital dance.

The miners pay for it, with their pocketbooks so full,

And hope the rewards are worth it, like a digital bull.

So if you ever hear about Proof of Work in play,

Remember, it's making the blockchain secure, day after day.

-The Simplified Explanation

Proof of Work is like a riddle that a group of friends has to solve before they can play a game. Imagine a group of friends who want to play a game of cards, but first, they have to solve a riddle. The riddle is challenging and requires a lot of brainpower to solve, but once they've solved it, they can start playing the game.

In a similar way, Proof of Work is a mathematical problem that a blockchain miner has to solve before they can add a new block to the chain. The mathematical problem is designed to be difficult to solve, but easy to verify once it's been solved. It requires a lot of computational power to solve, and the first miner to solve it gets to add the new block to the blockchain and receive a reward in the form of cryptocurrency.

The other miners on the network can then easily verify that the problem has been solved correctly, by checking the solution against the difficulty of the problem. This process of solving the mathematical problem is called Proof of Work, and it helps to ensure the security and integrity of the blockchain network.

-The Full Story

In this section, we will explore the Proof of Work (PoW) consensus mechanism used in the blockchain ecosystem. We will discuss the PoW algorithm, its advantages and disadvantages, and its role in securing the blockchain network.

-What Is Proof of Work?

Proof of Work is a consensus mechanism used in the blockchain ecosystem to validate transactions and add new blocks to the blockchain. In PoW, miners use computational power to solve complex mathematical problems, known as hash functions. The first miner to solve the hash function and validate the block is rewarded with cryptocurrency.

-PoW Algorithm

The PoW algorithm involves several steps, including:

1. Transaction Verification: Miners verify transactions on the network, ensuring that they are valid and meet the network's consensus rules.

2. Block Creation: Once a miner has validated a set of transactions, they combine them into a block and add a unique cryptographic signature to the block.

3. Solving the Hash Puzzle: Miners use specialized hardware and software to solve a complex mathematical puzzle known as a hash function. The first miner to solve the puzzle and add the block to the blockchain receives a reward.

4. Block Validation: Once a miner has solved the hash puzzle, other nodes on the network validate the block to ensure that it meets the network's consensus rules.

-Advantages of PoW

There are several advantages to using the PoW consensus mechanism in the blockchain ecosystem, including:

1. Security: PoW is a secure consensus mechanism, as it requires significant computational power to solve the hash function and add a block to the blockchain. This makes it difficult for malicious actors to alter the blockchain.

2. Decentralization: PoW allows for a decentralized network, as anyone with the necessary computational power can participate in the mining process.

3. Fairness: PoW is a fair consensus mechanism, as miners are rewarded based on their contribution to the network.

-Disadvantages of PoW

Despite its advantages, there are several disadvantages to using the PoW consensus mechanism, including:

1. Energy Consumption: PoW is an energy-intensive consensus mechanism, as it requires significant computational power to solve the hash function. This has led to concerns about the environmental impact of blockchain mining.

2. Centralization: PoW has the potential to become centralized, as miners with significant computational power may be able to control the network.

3. Slow Transactions: PoW can result in slow transaction times, as blocks can take several minutes or even hours to validate.

In conclusion, Proof of Work is a consensus mechanism used in the blockchain ecosystem to validate transactions and add new blocks to the blockchain. The PoW algorithm involves several steps, including transaction verification, block creation, solving the hash puzzle, and block validation.

PoW offers several advantages, including security, decentralization, and fairness, but it also has several disadvantages, including energy consumption, centralization, and slow transaction times. Understanding the PoW consensus mechanism is essential for understanding the overall operation and security of the blockchain network.

Chapter 9

Proof of Stake

-Poem

In the land of crypto, there's a proof so new,

That keeps the network secure, with a twist or two.

It's called Proof of Stake, and it's quite the fad,

Turning crypto ownership, into a competition so rad.

The stakers compete, with their coins so rare,

Locking them up in wallets, with digital care.

They use their ownership, to validate the chain,

And earn new coins as a reward, like a digital gain.

The stakers might get greedy, and hoard all their coins,

Or lose their keys, and end up with digital pains.

And then there's the rewards, that Proof of Stake provides,

The stakers earn new coins, like digital vibes.

They rely on the network, to keep the blockchain true,

And hope their investment pays off, like a digital coup.

So if you ever hear about Proof of Stake in play,

Remember, it's making the blockchain secure, day after day.

-The Simplified Explanation

Proof of Stake is like a group of friends who want to play a game of cards, and they each have to put up a deposit to ensure that they will play fairly. Imagine that each friend has to put some money into a pot before they can start playing. If they play the game fairly, they get their deposit back, but if they cheat, they lose their deposit.

In a similar way, Proof of Stake is a system in which blockchain validators, or "stakers," put up a deposit of cryptocurrency to validate new transactions on the network. Stakers are chosen at random to validate new transactions, and the amount of cryptocurrency they have deposited determines their chances of being chosen.

If a staker validates a transaction correctly, they earn a reward in the form of additional cryptocurrency. However, if they validate a transaction incorrectly or try to cheat the system, they lose their deposit. This incentivizes stakers to play fairly and ensures the security and integrity of the blockchain network. The more cryptocurrency a staker has deposited, the more likely they are to be chosen to validate new transactions, which makes the network more decentralized and secure.

-The Full Story

In this section, we will explore the Proof of stake (PoS) consensus mechanism used in the blockchain ecosystem. We will discuss the PoS algorithm, its advantages and disadvantages, and its role in securing the blockchain network.

-What Is Proof of Stake?

Proof of Stake is a consensus mechanism used in the blockchain ecosystem to validate transactions and add new blocks to the blockchain. In PoS, validators, also known as stakeholders, are selected to validate transactions and add new blocks to the blockchain based on the amount of cryptocurrency they hold.

-PoS Algorithm

The PoS algorithm involves several steps, including:

1. Validator Selection: Validators are selected to validate transactions and add new blocks to the blockchain based on the amount of cryptocurrency they hold. Validators are incentivized to behave honestly, as they risk losing their stake if they validate fraudulent transactions.

2. Transaction Verification: Validators verify transactions on the network, ensuring that they are valid and meet the network's consensus rules.

3. Block Creation: Once a validator has validated a set of transactions, they combine them into a block and add a unique cryptographic signature to the block.

4. Block Validation: Once a validator has created a block, other nodes on the network validate the block to ensure that it meets the network's consensus rules.

-Advantages of PoS

There are several advantages to using the PoS consensus mechanism in the blockchain ecosystem, including:

1. Energy Efficiency: PoS is an energy-efficient consensus mechanism, as it does not require significant computational power to validate transactions and add new blocks to the blockchain.

2. Decentralization: PoS allows for a decentralized network, as

anyone with a stake in the network can participate in the validation process.

3. Fairness: PoS is a fair consensus mechanism, as validators are selected based on the amount of cryptocurrency they hold, rather than their computational power.

-Disadvantages of PoS

Despite its advantages, there are several disadvantages to using the PoS consensus mechanism, including:

1. Centralization: PoS has the potential to become centralized, as validators with a significant amount of cryptocurrency may be able to control the network.

2. Staking Requirements: PoS requires participants to hold a significant amount of cryptocurrency, which may be a barrier to entry for some users.

3. Security: PoS may be less secure than PoW, as validators do not risk losing anything more than their stake if they validate fraudulent transactions.

In conclusion, Proof of Stake is a consensus mechanism used in the blockchain ecosystem to validate transactions and add new blocks to the blockchain. The PoS algorithm involves several steps, including validator selection, transaction verification, block creation, and block validation.

PoS offers several advantages, including energy efficiency, decentralization, and fairness, but it also has several disadvantages, including centralization, staking requirements, and potential security issues. Understanding the PoS consensus mechanism is essential for understanding the overall operation and security of the blockchain network.

Chapter 10

Hard Fork Vs Soft Fork

-poem

In the land of crypto, so strange and absurd,

A fork in the blockchain can leave you quite perturbed.

There are two types of forks, so listen up close.

One's hard, like a nut that won't crack,

The other's soft, like a pillow in the back.

A hard fork is when the chain splits in two,

Like trying to share a pizza with someone who hates you.

One chain goes this way, the other goes that,

And if you're not careful, your funds will go splat.

But a soft fork is different, it's more like a tweak,

Like adding a splash of milk to your coffee, so to speak.

The chain stays as one, with new rules to play,

Like giving miners more coins, to help them stay.

So when you're trading your coins and things start to shake,

Don't panic, my friend, it's just a blockchain break.

Just remember this poem, and you'll be just fine,

And maybe even chuckle at the thought of a fork in the line.

-Simplified Explanation

Let's say you have a book club that has certain rules for discussing and choosing books to read. One day, there is a disagreement among the members about the rules, and some members want to make significant changes to the rules while others want to keep them the same.

If the members who want to make significant changes decide to break away and form a new book club with entirely new rules, it would be like a hard fork in the blockchain. The new book club is separate and incompatible with the old club, and members who don't agree with the new rules can't participate in the new club.

On the other hand, if the members who want to make changes find a way to modify the existing rules so that they can coexist with the old rules, it would be like a soft fork in the blockchain. Members who haven't adopted the new rules can still participate in the book club, but those who have will be able to take advantage of new opportunities that the updated rules offer.

In summary, a hard fork is like forming a new club with different rules, while a soft fork is like tweaking the existing rules so that both old and new members can still participate together.

-The Full Story

A blockchain fork occurs when there is a permanent divergence in the blockchain's network, which can happen due to a change in its rules or protocol. Forks can be classified as either hard forks or soft forks, based on the degree of compatibility they have with the existing blockchain network.

A hard fork is a type of blockchain fork that creates a new blockchain network that is incompatible with the previous network. In a hard fork, the changes to the protocol are significant enough that nodes that are not updated to the new rules will no longer be able to validate transactions on the new blockchain. Hard forks typically occur when there is a fundamental disagreement among network participants about the direction of the blockchain or a major upgrade to the network's infrastructure. Hard forks can lead to the creation of new cryptocurrencies, as happened with Bitcoin Cash and Ethereum Classic.

On the other hand, a soft fork is a type of blockchain fork that is backward compatible with the existing network. In a soft fork, the changes to the protocol are not significant enough to create a new blockchain network, and nodes that have not upgraded their software can still validate transactions. Soft forks typically occur when there is a need to make minor changes to the network's rules or protocols. A common example of a soft fork is the Segregated Witness (SegWit) update in the Bitcoin network.

In summary, a hard fork creates a new, incompatible blockchain network, while a soft fork creates a backward compatible update to the existing network.

Chapter 11

Smart Contracts

-Poem

In the world of blockchain, there's a contract so smart,

That it can execute itself, like a work of art.

It's called a smart contract, and it's quite the sight,

Turning legal agreements, into a digital flight.

The contracts are like little programs, with code so tight,

They execute automatically, with no humans in sight.

They can transfer coins, or even digital rights,

And do it all securely, like a digital knight.

They might have a bug, or a glitch so small,

And end up doing something, not intended at all.

And then there's the code, that smart contracts require,

It takes lots of programming, like a digital choir.

The developers work hard, to make sure it's right,

And hope the contract works, like a digital might.

So if you ever hear about smart contracts in play,

Remember, they're making legal agreements, better each day.

-The Simplified Explanation

A smart contract is like a vending machine that automatically executes a transaction when certain conditions are met. Imagine you want to buy a can of soda from a vending machine. You put your money in, and if the machine detects that you've paid the correct amount, it dispenses the soda. A smart contract is similar, but instead of a vending machine, it's a computer program that executes automatically when certain conditions are met.

A smart contract is a self-executing program that runs on a blockchain network. It's written in code, and when certain conditions are met, the program automatically executes a transaction. For example, you could create a smart contract that pays out cryptocurrency to someone when they complete a certain task.

The contract is stored on the blockchain, and because it's executed automatically, there's no need for intermediaries or third parties to verify the transaction. This makes smart contracts efficient, secure, and transparent, and they have a wide range of potential applications, from financial transactions to supply chain management

-The Full Story

In this section, we will explore smart contracts and their role in the blockchain ecosystem. We will discuss what smart contracts are, how they work, and their potential applications.

-What Are Smart Contracts?

Smart contracts are self-executing contracts with the terms of the agreement written directly into lines of code. These contracts automatically execute when certain conditions are met, eliminating the need for intermediaries and reducing the risk of fraud and errors.

-How Do Smart Contracts Work?

Smart contracts work by executing code stored on the blockchain. The code contains the terms of the agreement and the logic to execute the agreement. The smart contract is triggered by an external event, such as the transfer of cryptocurrency, and automatically executes the terms of the agreement without the need for human intervention.

-Smart Contract Applications

Smart contracts have a wide range of applications, including:

1. Financial Contracts: Smart contracts can be used to execute financial contracts, such as options, futures, and swaps. These contracts can be executed automatically based on predefined conditions, reducing the need for intermediaries and increasing the speed and accuracy of the transaction.

2. Supply Chain Management: Smart contracts can be used to automate supply chain management, ensuring that products are delivered on time and that payment is made automatically when certain conditions are met.

3. Digital Identity: Smart contracts can be used to manage digital identities, allowing users to control their identity and personal data.

4. Real Estate: Smart contracts can be used to execute real estate contracts, such as property transfers and lease agreements. These contracts can be executed automatically based on predefined conditions, reducing the need for intermediaries and increasing the speed and accuracy of the transaction.

-Advantages of Smart Contracts

There are several advantages to using smart contracts, including:

1. Transparency: Smart contracts are transparent, as the terms of the agreement are stored on the blockchain and are visible to all parties involved in the transaction.

2. Trust: Smart contracts eliminate the need for intermediaries, reducing the risk of fraud and errors.

3. Efficiency: Smart contracts can be executed automatically based on predefined conditions, reducing the need for human intervention and increasing the speed and accuracy of the transaction.

-Disadvantages of Smart Contracts

Despite their advantages, there are several disadvantages to using smart contracts, including:

1. Code Errors: Smart contracts are only as reliable as the code they are written in. If there are errors in the code, the smart contract may not execute as intended, leading to unintended consequences.

2. Immutability: Smart contracts are immutable, meaning that once they are deployed to the blockchain, they cannot be changed. If there are errors in the code, they cannot be fixed.

3. Complexity: Smart contracts can be complex to write and understand, requiring expertise in programming and contract law.

In conclusion, smart contracts are self-executing contracts with the terms of the agreement written directly into lines of code. They automatically execute when certain conditions are met, eliminating the need for intermediaries and reducing the risk of fraud and errors.

Smart contracts have a wide range of applications, including financial contracts, supply chain management, digital identity, and real estate. While there are several advantages to using smart contracts, including transparency, trust, and efficiency, there are also several disadvantages, including code errors, immutability, and complexity. Understanding smart contracts is essential for understanding the potential applications and limitations of blockchain technology.

CONGRATULATIONS! You have made it through the fundamental concepts of Cryptocurrency and Blockchain Technology.

PART III -

A list of The Top Common Cryptocurrencies by Coin Market Cap

Chapter 1

Bitcoin (BTC)

Bitcoin is the world's first decentralized digital currency, which was created in 2009 by an unknown person or group under the pseudonym Satoshi Nakamoto. In this chapter, we will explore how Bitcoin works, how transactions are processed, and how the security of the Bitcoin network is maintained.

-The Bitcoin Network

The Bitcoin network is a decentralized peer-to-peer network, which means that there is no central authority or middleman controlling the network. Instead, transactions are processed and verified by network nodes called "miners," who are rewarded with newly created bitcoins for their work.

-How Transactions are Processed

When a user sends bitcoins to another user, the transaction is broadcast to the entire Bitcoin network. Miners then collect these transactions and add them to a "block" of transactions. Each block contains a unique code, called a "hash," which is generated by the miners based on the transactions in the block.

Once a block is generated, it is broadcast to the entire network, and other miners work to validate the transactions in the block. This process involves solving a complex mathematical puzzle, known as the "Proof of Work" algorithm. The first miner to solve the puzzle and validate the transactions in the block is rewarded with newly created bitcoins and fees from the transactions in the block.

-Security of the Bitcoin Network

The security of the Bitcoin network is maintained through the use of cryptography and the Proof of Work algorithm. Each transaction is verified using complex mathematical equations, which make it virtually impossible for anyone to tamper with the transactions.

Additionally, the Proof of Work algorithm ensures that the network is secure by making it extremely difficult and resource-intensive to generate new blocks. Miners must solve complex mathematical puzzles to validate transactions and generate new blocks, which requires a significant amount of computing power and energy.

-Bitcoin Wallets

Bitcoin wallets are digital wallets that store a user's private keys, which are used to access and transfer bitcoins. There are several types of Bitcoin wallets, including desktop wallets, mobile wallets, and hardware wallets.

Desktop and mobile wallets are software applications that run on a user's computer or mobile device, while hardware wallets are physical devices that store a user's private keys offline. Hardware wallets are considered to be the most secure type of Bitcoin wallet, as they are less vulnerable to hacking and cyberattacks.

In conclusion, Bitcoin is a decentralized digital currency that operates on a peer-to-peer network. Transactions are processed and validated by network nodes called miners, who are rewarded with newly created bitcoins for their work.

The security of the Bitcoin network is maintained through the use of cryptography and the proof of Work algorithm, which make it virtually impossible for anyone to tamper with the transactions.

Bitcoin wallets are digital wallets that store a user's private keys, which are used to access and transfer bitcoins. Understanding how Bitcoin works is essential for understanding the potential applications and limitations of blockchain technology.

Chapter 2

 **Ethereum (ETH)**

Ethereum is a decentralized blockchain platform that allows developers to build and deploy decentralized applications (dApps). In this chapter, we will explore how Ethereum works, how it differs from Bitcoin, and the role of smart contracts in the Ethereum ecosystem.

-The Ethereum Network

Like Bitcoin, the Ethereum network is a decentralized peer-to-peer network. However, unlike Bitcoin, which was designed primarily as a digital currency, Ethereum is designed as a platform for building decentralized applications.

In addition to the blockchain, the Ethereum network includes a virtual machine, called the Ethereum Virtual Machine (EVM), which allows developers to write and execute code on the blockchain. The EVM is a Turing-complete machine, which means that any program that can be written in any other programming language can be written in Ethereum's Solidity programming language and executed on the EVM.

-How Transactions Are Processed

When a user sends a transaction on the Ethereum network, it is broadcast to the entire network and processed by miners, who validate the transaction and add it to the blockchain. Each transaction on the

Ethereum network includes a "gas" limit and a "gas" price. Gas is the unit used to measure the computational effort required to execute a transaction or contract on the Ethereum network.

The gas limit is the maximum amount of gas that a user is willing to pay for the transaction, while the gas price is the amount of ether (the cryptocurrency of the Ethereum network) a user is willing to pay per unit of gas. The gas limit and gas price are used to calculate the total cost of the transaction, which is paid in ether. Miners are incentivized to process transactions by receiving a portion of the transaction fees in ether.

-Smart Contracts

Smart contracts are self-executing contracts with the terms of the agreement written into code. Smart contracts are stored on the Ethereum blockchain and can be executed by the EVM. They allow for the automation of complex agreements and transactions without the need for intermediaries.

Smart contracts are written in Solidity, a programming language specifically designed for the Ethereum network. Solidity allows developers to write complex programs, such as decentralized autonomous organizations (DAOs) and decentralized finance (DeFi) applications.

-Differences From Bitcoin

While Bitcoin and Ethereum are both decentralized blockchain networks, there are several key differences between the two.

1. First, Ethereum is designed as a platform for building decentralized applications, while Bitcoin is primarily a digital currency.

2. Additionally, while Bitcoin uses the Proof of Work algorithm to validate transactions and add them to the blockchain, Ethereum uses the Proof of Stake algorithm.

3. Finally, while Bitcoin has a fixed supply of 21 million coins, there is no fixed limit on the number of ether that can be created on the Ethereum network.

In conclusion, Ethereum is a decentralized blockchain platform that allows for the creation and deployment of decentralized applications. Transactions on the Ethereum network are processed by miners, who are incentivized with transaction fees paid in ether.

Smart contracts allow for the automation of complex agreements and transactions without the need for intermediaries. While Ethereum shares many similarities with Bitcoin, there are key differences between the two networks, including Ethereum's focus on dApp development and its use of a different consensus algorithm.

Chapter 3

 **Tether (USDT)**

Tether (USDT) is a stablecoin that has gained significant popularity among cryptocurrency traders and investors. Launched in 2014, it was one of the first stablecoins to hit the market, and has since become the most widely-used stablecoin, with a market capitalization of over $50 billion as of April 2023.

USDT is designed to maintain a stable value relative to the US dollar, with one USDT representing one US dollar in value. It achieves this stability by being backed by reserves of US dollars held in a bank account. For every USDT in circulation, there is supposed to be an equivalent amount of US dollars held in reserve.

The idea behind USDT is that it provides a way for traders to move funds between different cryptocurrency exchanges without having to convert their holdings into fiat currency. For example, a trader could buy USDT on one exchange using Bitcoin, and then transfer the USDT to another exchange where they could use it to buy other cryptocurrencies. This can be faster and cheaper than converting Bitcoin to fiat currency and then back into another cryptocurrency.

However, USDT has also been subject to controversy and criticism. One concern is that there may not be sufficient reserves of US dollars to back all of the USDT in circulation. Tether has claimed that all USDT is fully backed by reserves, but some critics have raised doubts about the transparency and legitimacy of Tether's reserves. Tether has faced legal challenges related to its reserves, including a settlement with the New York Attorney General's office in 2021.

Another criticism of USDT is that it may be used to manipulate the price of Bitcoin and other cryptocurrencies. Some traders have been accused of using USDT to artificially inflate the price of Bitcoin by buying large amounts of USDT and then using it to buy Bitcoin, creating the appearance of high demand for Bitcoin.

Despite these concerns, USDT remains a popular stablecoin in the cryptocurrency world. Its ability to maintain a stable value relative to the US dollar makes it a useful tool for traders and investors, and its widespread adoption means that it is easily accessible on most cryptocurrency exchanges.

However, it is important for users to be aware of the potential risks and controversies associated with USDT, and to make informed decisions when using it.

Chapter 4

BNB (BNB)

BNB (BNB) is the native cryptocurrency of the Binance exchange, one of the largest and most popular cryptocurrency exchanges in the world. Binance launched BNB in 2017 as part of its initial coin offering (ICO), and it has since become a major player in the cryptocurrency market, with a market capitalization of over $100 billion as of April 2023.

One of the main uses of BNB is to pay for trading fees on the Binance exchange. When traders use BNB to pay for fees, they receive a discount of up to 25% on the fees they would otherwise pay in Bitcoin or other cryptocurrencies. This makes BNB an attractive option for frequent traders who want to save money on fees.

In addition to its use as a fee payment option, BNB has also been used as a fundraising tool for blockchain projects through Binance Launchpad, a platform for hosting token sales. Projects that are selected for Launchpad can raise funds by selling their tokens for BNB. This has helped to fuel the growth of the Binance ecosystem, as successful projects are likely to attract new users and increase the trading volume on the exchange.

Another key feature of BNB is its use in the Binance Smart Chain (BSC), a blockchain platform that was launched by Binance in 2020. BNB is used as the primary fuel for transactions on the BSC, meaning that users must hold and use BNB to pay for transaction fees on the BSC. This has helped to drive demand for BNB and increase its value.

BNB also has other uses within the Binance ecosystem, such as being used to purchase virtual gifts on the Binance NFT marketplace and as collateral for borrowing on the Binance lending platform.

Despite its popularity and usefulness, BNB has not been without controversy. In 2021, the UK Financial Conduct Authority (FCA) issued a warning against Binance, citing concerns about its operations in the UK and the use of BNB as a fundraising tool. This led to a temporary dip in the value of BNB, but it has since recovered and continued to grow in value.

Overall, BNB has become an important cryptocurrency in the world of trading and blockchain projects, with a strong presence in the Binance ecosystem. Its utility and popularity suggest that it will continue to play an important role in the cryptocurrency market for years to come.

Chapter 5

 USD Coin (USDC)

USD Coin (USDC) is a stablecoin that is pegged to the US dollar, with one USDC representing one US dollar in value. It was launched in 2018 as a collaboration between Circle and Coinbase, two of the largest cryptocurrency companies in the world, and has since become one of the most widely-used stablecoins, with a market capitalization of over $40 billion as of April 2023.

Like other stablecoins, USDC is designed to provide a stable and predictable value for traders and investors. It achieves this stability by being fully backed by US dollars held in a bank account. For every USDC in circulation, there is supposed to be an equivalent amount of US dollars held in reserve.

USDC is also designed to be transparent and auditable, with regular audits conducted by third-party accounting firms to ensure that the reserves match the number of USDC in circulation. This level of transparency and accountability has helped to build trust among users and increase the adoption of USDC.

One of the key features of USDC is its integration with a wide range of cryptocurrency exchanges and platforms. It is available on most major exchanges and is used as a trading pair for a variety of cryptocurrencies, making it a versatile and useful tool for traders.

USDC is also used in decentralized finance (DeFi) applications, where it can be used to provide liquidity for lending and borrowing protocols, or as collateral for borrowing other cryptocurrencies. Its stability and widespread adoption make it a popular choice for these applications, as it provides a predictable value that can be used to mitigate price volatility in other cryptocurrencies.

In addition to its use in trading and DeFi, USDC is also used for payments and remittances. It can be sent and received quickly and easily, with low transaction fees, making it an attractive option for cross-border transactions and other use cases where traditional payment methods may be slow or expensive.

Overall, USDC has become a key player in the stablecoin market, offering a stable and transparent option for traders and investors, as well as a useful tool for DeFi applications and payments. Its popularity and wide adoption suggest that it will continue to play an important role in the cryptocurrency world for years to come.

Chapter 6

 XRP (XRP)

In the world of cryptocurrencies, XRP (XRP) has emerged as a game-changer for global payments. XRP is a digital currency that was created by Ripple Labs, a San Francisco-based fintech company, in 2012. Since then, XRP has grown to become one of the most popular and widely used cryptocurrencies in the world.

One of the key features of XRP is its speed of transaction processing. Unlike other cryptocurrencies that take minutes or even hours to confirm a transaction, XRP can settle transactions in just a few seconds. This makes XRP an ideal choice for cross-border payments, where speed and efficiency are crucial.

Another advantage of XRP is its low transaction fees. Compared to other cryptocurrencies like Bitcoin and Ethereum, which have high transaction fees due to the high demand and limited supply of block space, XRP has a negligible transaction fee. This makes XRP an attractive option for micropayments and other low-value transactions.

In addition to its speed and low fees, XRP also has the backing of major financial institutions. Ripple Labs has partnered with some of the biggest banks and payment providers in the world, including Santander, American Express, and Standard Chartered, to use XRP for cross-border payments. These partnerships have given XRP a level of legitimacy and acceptance in the financial industry that other cryptocurrencies have yet to achieve.

Despite its many advantages, XRP has also faced its fair share of challenges. In late 2020, the US Securities and Exchange Commission (SEC) filed a lawsuit against Ripple Labs, alleging that XRP was an unregistered security. This led to a sharp drop in the price of XRP and caused many exchanges to delist it from their platforms. The lawsuit is still ongoing, and its outcome could have significant implications for the future of XRP and the broader cryptocurrency industry.

Despite the challenges, the future of XRP looks bright. As the world becomes increasingly interconnected and the demand for fast and efficient cross-border payments grows, XRP is well-positioned to become the go-to cryptocurrency for global transactions. Its speed, low fees, and institutional backing make it a compelling choice for businesses and individuals alike.

In conclusion, XRP is a cryptocurrency that has the potential to revolutionize the way we make cross-border payments. With its speed, low fees, and institutional backing, XRP is well-positioned to become a major player in the global payments industry. While there are still challenges to overcome, the future of XRP looks bright and full of possibilities.

Chapter 7

 **Cardano (ADA)**

Cardano (ADA) is a third-generation blockchain platform that aims to provide a more secure, sustainable, and scalable infrastructure for decentralized applications and smart contracts. Launched in 2017, Cardano was created by a team of academics, developers, and engineers led by Charles Hoskinson, one of the co-founders of Ethereum.

One of the key features of Cardano is its Proof of Stake (PoS) consensus mechanism, which enables faster transaction processing and lower energy consumption compared to the Proof of Work (PoW) mechanism used by Bitcoin and many other cryptocurrencies. Cardano's PoS mechanism is called Ouroboros, and it uses a unique algorithm to randomly select validators who verify and confirm transactions on the network.

Another important aspect of Cardano is its focus on research and peer review. The development of Cardano is guided by a scientific approach, with a team of researchers and academics constantly studying and refining the protocol to ensure its security, scalability, and sustainability. Cardano also has a strong community of developers and enthusiasts who contribute to the project and help to build a thriving ecosystem of decentralized applications and services.

Cardano's native cryptocurrency, ADA, is used as a medium of exchange and a store of value on the network. Like Bitcoin and other cryptocurrencies, ADA can be used for peer-to-peer transactions and can be traded on cryptocurrency exchanges. However, Cardano also enables the creation of smart contracts and decentralized applications (dApps) that can be used for a variety of purposes, such as identity verification, supply chain management, and financial services.

One of the advantages of Cardano is its modular design, which allows for easy upgrades and improvements to the protocol without disrupting the entire network. Cardano is divided into two layers: the Cardano Settlement Layer (CSL) and the Cardano Computation Layer (CCL).

The CSL handles transactions and the distribution of ADA, while the CCL handles smart contracts and daApps. This separation of functions makes Cardano more flexible and adaptable to changing market conditions and user needs.

While Cardano is still relatively new and faces competition from other blockchain platforms, its unique features and scientific approach have made it an attractive option for developers and investors. Cardano has already seen significant growth in terms of market capitalization and adoption, and its potential for further growth and innovation is high.

In conclusion, Cardano is a third-generation blockchain platform that combines scientific rigor, modular design, and a focus on sustainability to provide a more secure, scalable, and flexible infrastructure for decentralized applications and smart contracts. With its PoS consensus mechanism, strong community, and commitment to research and development, Cardano is poised to become a major player in the blockchain industry and a key driver of innovation in the years to come.

Chapter 8

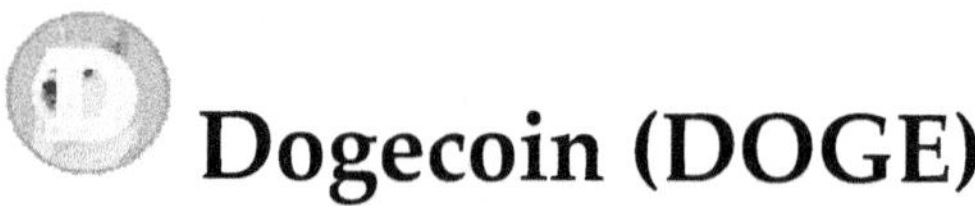 **Dogecoin (DOGE)**

Dogecoin is a decentralized, peer-to-peer cryptocurrency that was created in December 2013 by software developers Billy Markus and Jackson Palmer. The cryptocurrency was originally created as a joke, based on the popular "Doge" meme, which features a Shiba Inu dog with broken English captions. Despite its origins as a joke, Dogecoin has become a popular and valuable cryptocurrency, with a market capitalization of over $40 billion as of April 2023.

Dogecoin is based on the same code as Litecoin, a cryptocurrency that was created in 2011. It uses the Scrypt algorithm for mining, which is a memory-hard algorithm that is designed to be resistant to ASIC mining. Dogecoin has a block time of one minute, and a total supply of 129 billion coins, with new coins being created through mining rewards.

Dogecoin transactions are processed on a decentralized network, which is secured by a distributed network of miners. Transactions are validated through a POW consensus mechanism, which requires miners to solve complex mathematical problems in order to validate transactions and earn rewards.

-Advantages and Disadvantages

One of the main advantages of Dogecoin is its strong community and active development team. Dogecoin has a large and passionate community of users, who are active on social media and frequently use the cryptocurrency for charitable causes and community projects. Additionally, the Dogecoin development team has continued to update and improve the cryptocurrency over the years, with recent upgrades including the adoption of the AuxPoW (Auxiliary Proof of Work) algorithm, which allows Dogecoin miners to merge mine with Litecoin miners.

However, one of the disadvantages of Dogecoin is its lack of technical innovation. Unlike other cryptocurrencies, such as Bitcoin and Ethereum, which have introduced new and innovative features such as smart contracts and decentralized applications, Dogecoin has remained relatively unchanged since its creation in 2013. Additionally, Dogecoin's reliance on PoW mining has raised concerns about the environmental impact of the cryptocurrency, as mining requires a significant amount of energy and resources.

-Use Cases

Dogecoin is primarily used as a means of exchange and store of value, similar to other cryptocurrencies such as Bitcoin and Litecoin. However, Dogecoin's strong community and meme culture have also led to the creation of unique use cases, such as the "Doge4Water" campaign, which raised over $50,000 in Dogecoin to fund clean water initiatives in developing countries. Additionally, Dogecoin has been used to tip content creators on social media platforms such as Reddit and Twitter, as well as for charitable causes and community projects.

Dogecoin is a unique and popular cryptocurrency that has gained a large following thanks to its strong community and meme culture. While it may not have the technical innovation of other cryptocurrencies, Dogecoin's active development team and passionate community have helped it remain a popular and valuable asset in the cryptocurrency market.

However, as with any investment, it is important to understand the risks and potential drawbacks of investing in Dogecoin, and to carefully consider your own financial situation and investment goals before making any decisions.

Chapter 9

 Polygon (MATIC)

Polygon (MATIC) is a layer 2 scaling solution for Ethereum, designed to address the network's high gas fees and slow transaction processing times. It aims to provide faster and cheaper transactions while maintaining the security and decentralization of Ethereum.

Polygon was originally founded as Matic Network in 2017 by Jaynti Kanani, Sandeep Nailwal, and Anurag Arjun. The team's goal was to build a layer 2 scaling solution for Ethereum that would provide a better user experience, reduce congestion, and make dApps more accessible. In February 2021, the Matic Network rebranded as Polygon to reflect its expanding scope beyond just a scaling solution for Ethereum.

Polygon's architecture is built on top of Ethereum and allows for interoperability with other blockchain networks. It is an open-source, modular framework that offers several components, including Polygon software development kit (SDK), Polygon POS Chain, Polygon AMM, Polygon PoS Bridge, and Polygon Plasma.

The Polygon SDK provides developers with tools to build dApps that can be deployed on the Polygon network. It supports Ethereum Virtual Machine (EVM) and Web3.js, making it easy for developers to migrate their existing Ethereum dApps to Polygon. The Polygon POS Chain is the main component of Polygon's architecture and serves as a layer 2 scaling solution for Ethereum. It uses a Proof of Stake (PoS) consensus mechanism to validate transactions, reducing the energy consumption required for mining on the Ethereum network.

Polygon AMM (Automated Market Maker) is a decentralized exchange (DEX) that allows users to trade cryptocurrencies in a trustless and permissionless manner. It uses an algorithm to determine the prices of assets and provides liquidity through automated trading pools. Polygon PoS Bridge enables seamless transfers of assets between Ethereum and Polygon networks.

The Polygon Plasma component is a scaling solution for dApps that require high throughput and low latency. It uses a sidechain construction to facilitate off-chain transactions, reducing congestion on the Ethereum network. Polygon Plasma supports Ethereum smart contracts and allows developers to build scalable and secure dApps.

Polygon's native token, MATIC, is used as a utility token to pay for transactions and fees on the network. It can also be staked to participate in network validation and earn rewards. In addition to staking, MATIC can be used for governance on the Polygon network, allowing token holders to vote on proposals and influence network decisions.

Polygon has gained significant attention and adoption in the blockchain space, with several high-profile partnerships and integrations with projects such as Aave, Chainlink, and Decentraland. It has also attracted several notable investors, including Mark Cuban, who announced in May 2021 that he had invested in the project.

In conclusion, Polygon (MATIC) has emerged as a promising layer 2 scaling solution for Ethereum, offering faster and cheaper transactions without sacrificing the security and decentralization of the network. With a growing ecosystem of dApps, developers, and investors, Polygon is poised to play a significant role in the future of blockchain technology.

Chapter 10

 Solana (SOL)

Solana (SOL) is a high-performance blockchain that has been gaining traction in the cryptocurrency world due to its impressive speed and low transaction fees. Built by a team of seasoned blockchain engineers, Solana has quickly become one of the most exciting blockchain projects in the space.

The Solana blockchain was created to address the scalability issues that many other blockchains, such as Ethereum, have struggled with. Solana's unique architecture allows it to process up to 65,000 transactions per second, making it one of the fastest blockchains in the world. This is accomplished through the use of a novel consensus mechanism called Proof of History (PoH) and a network of parallel blockchains called "shards."

Proof of History is a mechanism that allows nodes on the Solana network to verify the order of transactions without having to process them. This significantly reduces the amount of time it takes for a transaction to be confirmed, as nodes no longer have to wait for other nodes to process the transaction before verifying its order. By using Proof of History, Solana is able to achieve high transaction throughput while maintaining a high level of security and decentralization.

In addition to Proof of History, Solana also uses a network of parallel blockchains called shards to further increase its transaction throughput. Each shard is capable of processing transactions independently, allowing for more transactions to be processed simultaneously. Sharding is a common technique used in other blockchain projects, but Solana's implementation is unique in that it allows shards to communicate with each other seamlessly, ensuring that the network remains cohesive and secure.

Solana's speed and scalability make it an ideal blockchain for decentralized applications (dApps) and other use cases that require fast and inexpensive transactions. Solana's low transaction fees, which are currently around $0.0001 per transaction, make it one of the most affordable blockchains to use. This has led to a growing number of projects building on the Solana blockchain, including some high-profile projects like Serum, Mango Markets, and Raydium.

The Solana team has also been actively working on expanding the capabilities of the Solana ecosystem. In addition to building out the core blockchain infrastructure, the Solana team has developed a number of tools and services to help developers build and deploy applications on the Solana network. These include a software development kit (SDK), a wallet, and a decentralized exchange (DEX).

The future of Solana looks promising, as the project continues to gain traction and attract new users and developers to its ecosystem. With its impressive speed and low transaction fees, Solana has the potential to become a major player in the blockchain space and drive innovation in decentralized finance (DeFi), gaming, and other areas of the decentralized web.

Chapter 11

 **Polkadot (DOT)**

Polkadot (DOT) is a next-generation blockchain protocol that aims to address the issue of interoperability between different blockchains. Developed by Gavin Wood, one of the co-founders of Ethereum, Polkadot is designed to allow for the seamless exchange of data and assets between different blockchain networks.

At its core, Polkadot is a multi-chain network that allows different blockchains to communicate with each other using a common language. This is accomplished through the use of a relay chain, which acts as the main hub for the Polkadot network, and a series of parachains, which are specialized blockchains that can be tailored to specific use cases.

The relay chain is responsible for maintaining the security and consensus of the entire Polkadot network, while the parachains can be customized to support a variety of different applications and use cases. This modular design allows for greater flexibility and scalability, as new parachains can be added to the network as needed without affecting the overall performance or security of the network.

One of the key advantages of Polkadot is its ability to facilitate cross-chain communication and interoperability. This is achieved through the use of a messaging protocol called the Polkadot Cross-Chain Message Passing (XCMP) protocol. The XCMP protocol allows different parachains to communicate with each other and share data and assets in a secure and decentralized manner.

Polkadot's focus on interoperability has made it a popular choice for developers and projects looking to build decentralized applications (dApps) and other blockchain-based solutions. The Polkadot ecosystem has already attracted a number of high-profile projects, including Acala, Moonbeam, and Chainlink, all of which are building on the Polkadot network.

Another unique feature of Polkadot is its governance mechanism. Polkadot is designed to be a fully decentralized and community-driven network, with decisions about the future development and direction of the network made through a process of on-chain governance. This allows stakeholders to vote on proposals and changes to the network, ensuring that the community has a say in the evolution of the platform.

The future of Polkadot looks bright, as the project continues to gain momentum and attract new developers and users to its ecosystem. With its focus on interoperability and modularity, Polkadot has the potential to become a key player in the blockchain space, enabling new levels of innovation and collaboration between different blockchain networks.

As the world becomes more decentralized, the need for interoperability and collaboration between different blockchain networks will only continue to grow, and Polkadot is well-positioned to meet this need.

Chapter 12

Binance USD (BUSD)

Binance USD (BUSD) is a stablecoin that is pegged to the value of the U.S. dollar. Stablecoins like BUSD are designed to provide the benefits of cryptocurrencies, such as fast transaction times and low fees, while also maintaining a stable value that is not subject to the same price volatility as other cryptocurrencies like Bitcoin and Ethereum.

Stablecoins are becoming an increasingly popular option for cryptocurrency traders and investors, as they provide a way to move funds quickly and easily between different cryptocurrency exchanges without having to worry about fluctuations in value. They also offer a way to hedge against market volatility, as stablecoins can be exchanged for fiat currencies like the U.S. dollar at a 1:1 ratio.

BUSD was created by Binance, one of the largest cryptocurrency exchanges in the world. The stablecoin was launched in September 2019 and is now available on a number of different exchanges, including Binance, Coinbase, and Gemini. One of the key benefits of BUSD is its transparency and regulatory compliance. Unlike some other stablecoins that have faced questions about their reserves and backing, BUSD is fully backed by U.S. dollars held in FDIC-insured bank accounts. This provides users with peace of mind, as they can be confident that their BUSD tokens are backed by actual dollars held in secure and regulated institutions.

BUSD also offers fast transaction times and low fees, making it an attractive option for cryptocurrency traders and investors. Transactions on the Binance Smart Chain, which supports BUSD, can be completed in just a few seconds, and fees are typically much lower than those associated with other cryptocurrencies. Another advantage of BUSD is its integration with the Binance ecosystem. Binance offers a wide range of cryptocurrency trading and investment options, and BUSD can be used to trade on the Binance exchange or to participate in other Binance-related products and services.

Looking to the future, stablecoins like BUSD are likely to play an increasingly important role in the cryptocurrency landscape. As more individuals and institutions seek to enter the crypto market, the need for stable and secure options for buying, selling, and storing cryptocurrency will only continue to grow. With its strong regulatory compliance, transparency, and integration with the Binance ecosystem, BUSD is well-positioned to meet this growing demand for stable and reliable cryptocurrency options.

Chapter 13

 Litecoin (LTC)

Litecoin (LTC) is a peer-to-peer cryptocurrency that was created in 2011 by Charlie Lee, a former Google engineer. Like Bitcoin, Litecoin is based on a decentralized, open-source protocol that enables fast, secure, and low-cost transactions without the need for intermediaries such as banks or payment processors.

One of the key features of Litecoin is its faster block generation time compared to Bitcoin. While Bitcoin blocks are generated every 10 minutes, Litecoin blocks are generated every 2.5 minutes, which means transactions can be confirmed and settled much faster on the Litecoin network. This makes Litecoin a more practical option for everyday transactions and micropayments. Another advantage of Litecoin is its lower transaction fees compared to Bitcoin. While Bitcoin fees can sometimes be high due to network congestion, Litecoin fees are usually much lower, making it an attractive option for people who want to avoid high fees and slow transaction times.

Litecoin is often referred to as the digital silver to Bitcoin's digital gold, due to its similarities to Bitcoin and its focus on being a practical, everyday cryptocurrency. Litecoin has a fixed maximum supply of 84 million coins, which is four times the maximum supply of Bitcoin. This means that Litecoin has a lower value per coin, but it also means that it has a greater potential for wider adoption and usage.

In addition to its practicality and low fees, Litecoin also has a strong community of developers and enthusiasts who contribute to its development and adoption. Litecoin has been around for over a decade and has withstood the test of time, making it a reliable and trusted cryptocurrency.

While Litecoin faces competition from other cryptocurrencies, it has a loyal following and a solid track record. Litecoin has been used for a variety of purposes, from everyday transactions to fundraising for charitable causes. Its fast transaction times, low fees, and strong community make it a promising option for people who want a practical and reliable cryptocurrency for their everyday needs.

In conclusion, Litecoin is a peer-to-peer cryptocurrency that was created to provide a faster, more practical alternative to Bitcoin. With its faster block generation time, lower transaction fees, and strong community, Litecoin has emerged as a reliable and trusted cryptocurrency that has the potential for wider adoption and usage. While there are challenges and competition in the cryptocurrency market, Litecoin's track record and loyal following make it a promising option for the future.

Chapter 14

 Shiba Inu (SHIB)

Shiba Inu (SHIB) is a decentralized, peer-to-peer cryptocurrency that was created in August 2020. It is an ERC-20 token on the Ethereum blockchain, and was created as a "Dogecoin killer" in reference to the popular Dogecoin cryptocurrency. SHIB is part of a group of "meme coins" that have gained popularity due to their unique branding and strong online communities. SHIB is built on the Ethereum blockchain, which is a decentralized, open-source blockchain platform that allows developers to build decentralized applications (dApps) and smart contracts. As an ERC-20 token, SHIB can be stored in any Ethereum wallet that supports ERC-20 tokens, such as MyEtherWallet or MetaMask.

SHIB has a total supply of 1 quadrillion tokens, which is significantly larger than most other cryptocurrencies. The large supply is designed to keep the price of each individual token low, making it more accessible to a wider range of investors. SHIB transactions are processed on the Ethereum network, which is secured by a distributed network of miners.

-Advantages and Disadvantages

One of the main advantages of SHIB is its strong online community and active development team. SHIB has gained a large following on social media platforms such as Twitter and Reddit, with users frequently engaging in community projects and charitable causes. Additionally, the SHIB development team has continued to update and improve the cryptocurrency over time, with recent upgrades, including the launch of ShibaSwap, a decentralized exchange that allows users to trade SHIB and other cryptocurrencies.

However, one of the disadvantages of SHIB is its lack of technical innovation. While it shares some similarities with other cryptocurrencies, such as Ethereum and Bitcoin, SHIB does not introduce any new or innovative features. Additionally, the large supply of SHIB tokens has raised concerns about the potential for inflation and market manipulation, as large holders of the cryptocurrency could potentially manipulate the market by selling off their holdings.

-Use Cases

SHIB is primarily used as a means of exchange and store of value, similar to other cryptocurrencies. However, the strong online community and meme culture surrounding SHIB have led to the creation of unique use cases, such as the "WoofPaper" project, which aims to create a decentralized marketplace for buying and selling digital art using SHIB and other cryptocurrencies. Additionally, SHIB has been used to tip content creators on social media platforms such as Twitter and TikTok, as well as for charitable causes and community projects.

SHIB is a unique and popular cryptocurrency that has gained a large following thanks to its strong online community and unique branding. While it may not have the technical innovation of other cryptocurrencies, SHIB's active development team and passionate community have helped it remain a popular asset in the cryptocurrency market.

However, as with any investment, it is important to understand the risks and potential drawbacks of investing in SHIB, and to carefully consider your own financial situation and investment goals before making any decisions.

Chapter 15

 TRONIX (TRX)

TRON (TRX) is a blockchain-based platform founded in September 2017 by Justin Sun, a young Chinese entrepreneur. The platform aims to decentralize the internet by creating a global, open-source, and decentralized content entertainment system. TRON aims to eliminate intermediaries and empower users to create, share, and own content without the interference of third parties. The platform provides a range of tools and services to support the development of decentralized applications (dApps) that leverage blockchain technology to deliver content and services directly to users.

TRON has a robust and active community, which has helped the platform to grow significantly since its inception. The platform's native cryptocurrency, TRONIX (TRX), is used to power transactions on the network, and it can be used to pay for content and services on the platform.

TRON has its own blockchain, which is based on the Delegated Proof of Stake (DPoS) consensus mechanism. This mechanism allows users to vote for super representatives who validate transactions on the network. The TRON blockchain is scalable, with a capacity to process up to 2,000 transactions per second.

The TRON platform supports the development of decentralized

applications through its TRON Virtual Machine (TVM). The TVM is a lightweight, Turing-complete virtual machine that allows developers to build and deploy smart contracts on the TRON network. Smart contracts are self-executing contracts that can automate complex processes and transactions, enabling a range of decentralized services to be built on the TRON platform.

TRON also supports the creation of custom tokens through its TRC-20 token standard. This standard allows developers to create their own tokens on the TRON network, which can be used for a variety of purposes, such as fundraising or creating loyalty programs.

TRON's ecosystem includes a wide range of decentralized applications, including social media platforms, gaming applications, music streaming platforms, and more. Some of the most popular dApps on the TRON network include BitTorrent, TRONbet, and WINk. These dApps are powered by the TRON blockchain and provide users with a range of decentralized services.

TRON has also made significant progress in terms of partnerships and collaborations. The platform has formed partnerships with several companies in the entertainment industry, including the BitTorrent peer-to-peer file sharing network and the Opera web browser. These partnerships have helped to increase the visibility and adoption of the TRON platform.

In conclusion, TRON is a blockchain-based platform that aims to decentralize the internet by creating a global, open-source, and decentralized content entertainment system. The platform provides a range of tools and services to support the development of decentralized applications (dApps) that leverage blockchain technology to deliver content and services directly to users. With its dedicated team, strong community, and ambitious roadmap, TRON has the potential to become a major player in the blockchain industry in the years to come.

Chapter 16

 Avalanche (AVAX)

Avalanche (AVAX) is a blockchain-based platform founded in 2018 by Emin Gün Sirer, a renowned computer scientist and blockchain researcher. The platform aims to provide fast, efficient, and highly scalable decentralized solutions to its users. Avalanche seeks to address the issues of slow transaction speeds and high fees that have plagued other blockchain networks, making it an attractive option for decentralized finance (DeFi) and other applications that require high throughput and low latency.

Avalanche is built on a consensus mechanism called Avalanche Consensus, which is a novel consensus mechanism that allows for extremely fast and secure transactions. Avalanche Consensus is a variation of the Proof of Stake (PoS) consensus mechanism, which allows users to participate in the validation of transactions on the network by staking their AVAX tokens.

Avalanche supports the creation of custom tokens through its Avalanche Standard Asset (ASA) protocol, which allows developers to create and issue their own tokens on the Avalanche network. These tokens can be used for a wide range of applications, including fundraising, reward programs, and gaming.

Avalanche also supports the development of decentralized applications (dApps) through its Avalanche-X program, which provides resources and support to developers building on the Avalanche network. Avalanche-X provides developers with access to tools, resources, and technical assistance to help them build and launch dApps on the Avalanche network.

One of the key features of Avalanche is its subnets architecture, which allows for the creation of independent blockchain networks that can operate within the Avalanche ecosystem. Subnets can have their own validators, consensus rules, and token economies, making it possible to create customized blockchain networks for specific use cases.

Another key feature of Avalanche is its interoperability with other blockchain networks. Avalanche is designed to be compatible with Ethereum, allowing developers to port their Ethereum-based dApps to the Avalanche network easily. Avalanche also supports the creation of bridges to other blockchain networks, which can facilitate the transfer of assets and data between different blockchain ecosystems.

In terms of governance, Avalanche is a decentralized network that is governed by its community of stakeholders. AVAX token holders have the right to vote on proposals related to network upgrades, network fees, and other important decisions affecting the network.

In conclusion, Avalanche is a high-performance blockchain network that is designed to provide fast, efficient, and highly scalable decentralized solutions to its users. With its novel consensus mechanism, support for custom tokens and dApps, interoperability with other blockchain networks, and strong governance model, Avalanche is well-positioned to become a major player in the blockchain industry in the years to come.

Chapter 17

 **Dai (DAI)**

Dai (DAI) is a decentralized stablecoin that operates on the Ethereum blockchain. The stablecoin was launched in 2017 by MakerDAO, a decentralized autonomous organization that governs the creation and management of the Dai stablecoin.

Dai is designed to maintain a stable value of 1 USD, unlike other cryptocurrencies that experience volatile price fluctuations. Dai achieves price stability by being collateralized by other cryptocurrencies such as Ether (ETH), which are locked up in smart contracts on the Ethereum blockchain.

To generate Dai, users must first deposit their cryptocurrency holdings as collateral in the MakerDAO smart contract. The amount of Dai that can be generated depends on the value of the collateral deposited, as well as a collateralization ratio that is set by MakerDAO. The collateralization ratio represents the amount of collateral required to generate a certain amount of Dai, and it is set to ensure that the value of the collateral is always greater than the value of the generated Dai.

Once Dai is generated, it can be used as a stable store of value, a medium of exchange, or a unit of account. Dai is fully decentralized, meaning that it is not controlled by any single entity, and it can be transferred and traded freely on the Ethereum blockchain.

Dai has a number of advantages over traditional fiat-backed stablecoins. Firstly, Dai is completely decentralized, meaning that it is not subject to the same regulatory and censorship risks as fiat-backed stablecoins. Secondly, Dai can be generated and traded without the need for a central authority or trusted third party. This makes Dai more accessible to users who may not have access to traditional financial institutions.

In addition to its stability, Dai is also highly interoperable with other decentralized applications on the Ethereum blockchain. Dai can be used as a medium of exchange for a wide range of decentralized services, such as decentralized exchanges, lending platforms, and prediction markets.

To maintain the stability of the Dai stablecoin, MakerDAO regularly adjusts the collateralization ratio and issues new MKR tokens through a decentralized governance process. MKR token holders have the ability to vote on proposals related to the management of the Dai stablecoin, including changes to the collateralization ratio and the issuance of new MKR tokens.

In conclusion, Dai is a decentralized stablecoin that provides a stable store of value and medium of exchange on the Ethereum blockchain. With its collateralized model, interoperability with other decentralized applications, and decentralized governance model, Dai has emerged as a popular stablecoin in the decentralized finance (DeFi) ecosystem.

Chapter 18

Wrapped Bitcoin (WBTC)

Wrapped Bitcoin (WBTC) is an ERC-20 token that is pegged to the value of Bitcoin (BTC). It is a collaboration between several decentralized finance (DeFi) projects, including BitGo, Kyber Network, and Ren, that allows users to access the functionality of Bitcoin while taking advantage of the benefits of the Ethereum blockchain.

The concept behind WBTC is simple. BTC holders deposit their Bitcoin into a custodian, which then mints an equivalent amount of WBTC on the Ethereum blockchain. The WBTC tokens are then held in a smart contract and can be transferred and traded just like any other ERC-20 token.

WBTC provides a number of benefits over traditional Bitcoin. Firstly, it enables BTC holders to participate in the growing DeFi ecosystem. By holding WBTC, users can access a wide range of DeFi applications, such as decentralized exchanges, lending platforms, and yield farming protocols. These applications are not available to BTC holders because the Bitcoin blockchain is not designed to support smart contracts.

Secondly, WBTC is faster and cheaper to use than Bitcoin. Transactions on the Ethereum blockchain are generally faster and less expensive than transactions on the Bitcoin blockchain. This means that users can transfer and trade WBTC more quickly and at a lower cost than BTC.

WBTC is also more flexible than Bitcoin. By being an ERC-20 token, WBTC can be integrated with other Ethereum-based projects, such as wallets and payment systems. This enables users to use WBTC in a wider range of applications and use cases.

Finally, WBTC is more transparent than Bitcoin. The WBTC smart contract is fully audited and transparent, meaning that users can easily verify the amount of Bitcoin backing each WBTC token. This is important because it ensures that each WBTC token is fully backed by an equivalent amount of Bitcoin.

To ensure the transparency and security of the WBTC system, the token is governed by a consortium of decentralized organizations, including BitGo, Kyber Network, and Ren. These organizations are responsible for the management of the WBTC system, including the minting and burning of WBTC tokens.

In conclusion, Wrapped Bitcoin (WBTC) is a bridge between the Bitcoin and Ethereum ecosystems that allows Bitcoin holders to access the functionality of the Ethereum blockchain. By providing faster, cheaper, and more flexible access to Bitcoin, WBTC has emerged as a popular option for users looking to participate in the growing DeFi ecosystem.

Chapter 19

 Chainlink (LINK)

Chainlink (LINK) is a decentralized oracle network that aims to connect smart contracts on the blockchain to real-world data and events. It was founded in 2017 by Sergey Nazarov and Steve Ellis, and is currently one of the most widely used oracle networks in the blockchain ecosystem.

Smart contracts are self-executing contracts that operate on the blockchain. They are designed to execute automatically when certain conditions are met, without the need for intermediaries or human intervention. However, smart contracts currently have limited access to external data and events, which limits their functionality.

This is where Chainlink comes in. The Chainlink network provides a secure and decentralized way to access off-chain data and events, such as stock prices, weather data, and sports scores, and make it available to smart contracts on the blockchain. This allows smart contracts to make decisions based on real-world data, and enables the creation of more complex and sophisticated decentralized applications.

Chainlink achieves this by using a decentralized network of oracles, which are trusted sources of data that provide information to smart contracts. Oracles are independent entities that are incentivized to provide accurate data, and they are selected based on their reputation, reliability, and performance.

The Chainlink network also uses a unique consensus mechanism called the "LINK token staking" system. In this system, node operators, who provide the necessary computing power and resources to run the Chainlink network, must stake a certain amount of LINK tokens. This creates an economic incentive for node operators to provide accurate data, as they risk losing their stake if they provide incorrect information.

One of the key benefits of Chainlink is its ability to provide secure and reliable data to smart contracts. This is achieved through the use of tamper-proof hardware security modules (HSMs) that are used to store private keys and sign data. This ensures that data cannot be manipulated or altered, and provides a high level of security for smart contract applications.

Chainlink has been adopted by a wide range of blockchain projects, including DeFi protocols, prediction markets, and gaming applications. It is widely regarded as one of the most important infrastructure projects in the blockchain ecosystem, and has gained a large following among developers and users alike.

In conclusion, Chainlink (LINK) is a decentralized oracle network that provides a secure and reliable way to connect smart contracts on the blockchain to real-world data and events. With its decentralized network of oracles, unique consensus mechanism, and tamper-proof security features, Chainlink has emerged as a key infrastructure project in the blockchain ecosystem.

Chapter 20

 Uniswap (UNI)

Uniswap (UNI) is a decentralized cryptocurrency exchange (DEX) that allows users to trade cryptocurrencies without the need for intermediaries or a centralized order book. It was founded in 2018 by Hayden Adams, and is built on the Ethereum blockchain.

The Uniswap protocol is powered by smart contracts, which are self-executing contracts that operate on the blockchain. Unlike traditional centralized exchanges, which require users to deposit funds into a centralized wallet, Uniswap allows users to trade cryptocurrencies directly from their own wallets. This means that users always maintain control of their funds and are not subject to the security risks of a centralized exchange.

The Uniswap exchange uses an automated market maker (AMM) model, which uses mathematical formulas to determine the price of a cryptocurrency based on its supply and demand. This eliminates the need for a centralized order book and allows for instant trades at any time, without the need for matching buyers and sellers.

In the Uniswap AMM model, liquidity providers (LPs) provide pairs of cryptocurrencies to a liquidity pool, which is used to facilitate trades on the exchange. LPs earn a portion of the trading fees generated by the liquidity pool in proportion to their contribution. This incentivizes users to provide liquidity to the exchange, which helps to increase liquidity and reduce slippage.

Uniswap has also introduced its own native token, UNI, which was launched in September 2020. UNI is used to govern the Uniswap protocol and allows holders to participate in the decision-making process for the future development of the exchange. It is also used to incentivize users to provide liquidity to the exchange, by rewarding them with UNI tokens for their contributions.

Since its launch, Uniswap has become one of the most widely used DEXs in the cryptocurrency ecosystem, and has played a significant role in the growth of the decentralized finance (DeFi) movement. It has been adopted by a wide range of DeFi projects, and has facilitated billions of dollars in trading volume.

In conclusion, Uniswap (UNI) is a decentralized cryptocurrency exchange that uses an automated market maker model to facilitate trades without the need for intermediaries or a centralized order book. With its focus on user control and incentivized liquidity provision, Uniswap has emerged as one of the most important projects in the DeFi ecosystem.

Chapter 21

 Monero (XMR)

Monero (XMR) is a decentralized, privacy-focused cryptocurrency that was launched in 2014. It is built on the principles of privacy, security, and fungibility, and aims to provide a secure and untraceable way to conduct transactions online.

One of the key features of Monero is its focus on privacy. Unlike other cryptocurrencies, such as Bitcoin, Monero uses a unique technology called "ring signatures" to obfuscate the sender and receiver of transactions, as well as the amount being transacted. This makes it very difficult to trace transactions back to their original source, ensuring a high level of privacy for Monero users.

In addition to ring signatures, Monero also uses stealth addresses, which allow users to generate multiple one-time use addresses for each transaction. This makes it even more difficult to trace transactions, as each transaction appears to be sent to a unique address.

Monero also has a dynamic block size, which means that the size of each block is adjusted automatically based on the amount of transactions being processed. This ensures that the Monero network can handle a large volume of transactions without becoming congested or slowing down.

Another important feature of Monero is its focus on fungibility.

Fungibility refers to the ability of a currency or asset to be exchanged for another unit of the same currency or asset, without any difference in value. Monero ensures fungibility by ensuring that each unit of XMR is interchangeable with any other unit, regardless of its transaction history.

In terms of mining, Monero uses a Proof of Work (PoW) consensus algorithm, which is used to validate transactions and generate new XMR coins. However, unlike Bitcoin, Monero uses a unique mining algorithm called "RandomX," which is designed to be ASIC-resistant. This means that mining on Monero can be done using a regular computer or laptop, making it more accessible to a wider range of users.

Monero has been adopted by a wide range of users and businesses, and is often used for transactions that require a high level of privacy and security, such as online purchases and donations to charities or political campaigns.

In conclusion, Monero (XMR) is a decentralized, privacy-focused cryptocurrency that offers a high level of anonymity and fungibility. With its use of unique technologies such as ring signatures and stealth addresses, Monero has become one of the most widely used privacy-focused cryptocurrencies in the cryptocurrency ecosystem.

Chapter 22

 **Ethereum Classic (ETC)**

Ethereum Classic (ETC) is a decentralized, open-source blockchain platform that was created in 2016 as a result of a hard fork from the original Ethereum (ETH) blockchain. The split occurred as a result of disagreements within the Ethereum community over the handling of a high-profile hacking incident.

Like Ethereum, Ethereum Classic allows developers to build decentralized applications (dapps) and smart contracts using a programming language called Solidity. However, unlike Ethereum, Ethereum Classic is designed to operate as a more decentralized and immutable blockchain platform, with a focus on maintaining the original principles of blockchain technology.

One of the key features of Ethereum Classic is its focus on immutability. This means that once a transaction has been recorded on the Ethereum Classic blockchain, it cannot be changed or reversed. This ensures that the integrity of the blockchain is maintained and that the transactions recorded on the blockchain are secure and transparent.

Ethereum Classic also uses a Proof of Work (PoW) consensus algorithm, similar to Bitcoin, which is used to validate transactions and add new blocks to the blockchain. This process is carried out by miners, who use specialized hardware to solve complex mathematical problems in order to validate transactions and earn ETC rewards.

Another important feature of Ethereum Classic is its focus on interoperability. This means that Ethereum Classic is designed to work with other blockchain platforms and to facilitate the transfer of assets between different blockchains. This is achieved through the use of cross-chain bridges and interoperability protocols, which allow different blockchain platforms to communicate with each other and to exchange assets.

Since its creation, Ethereum Classic has been adopted by a wide range of developers and businesses, and has been used to build a variety of decentralized applications and blockchain-based solutions. It has also been listed on a wide range of cryptocurrency exchanges, making it easily accessible to users around the world.

In conclusion, Ethereum Classic (ETC) is a decentralized, open-source blockchain platform that offers a focus on immutability, decentralization, and interoperability. With its use of Proof of Work consensus and a focus on maintaining the original principles of blockchain technology, Ethereum Classic has become a popular blockchain platform for developers and businesses alike.

Chapter 23

Bitcoin Cash (BTC)

Bitcoin Cash (BCH) is a decentralized digital currency that was created in 2017 as a result of a hard fork of the Bitcoin (BTC) blockchain. A hard fork is a significant change to a blockchain's protocol that creates a new blockchain with separate rules and features from the original blockchain. The hard fork was created in response to the scaling debate within the Bitcoin community, which involved disagreement on how to increase the network's capacity to handle more transactions. Bitcoin Cash was created with the intention of addressing the scaling issues that Bitcoin was facing.

Bitcoin Cash has a similar design and architecture to Bitcoin, as it is based on the same open-source code and uses a consensus mechanism based on proof-of-work mining. However, Bitcoin Cash has several distinct features that differentiate it from Bitcoin, including a larger block size limit of 32 MB (compared to Bitcoin's 1 MB limit) and a different difficulty adjustment algorithm.

The larger block size limit enables Bitcoin Cash to handle more transactions per second than Bitcoin. Additionally, Bitcoin Cash has lower transaction fees and faster confirmation times than Bitcoin due to its larger block size limit.

Bitcoin Cash is often seen as a currency that is more suitable for everyday use compared to Bitcoin. It is accepted by a growing number of merchants and can be used for online purchases, remittances, and peer-to-peer transactions.

Overall, Bitcoin Cash aims to provide a fast, low-cost, and reliable cryptocurrency that can be used for day-to-day transactions. While it shares similarities with Bitcoin, it has a distinct identity and set of features that make it an attractive alternative for individuals and businesses alike.

PART IV -

The Future of Blockchain and Crypto; Tips to keep In Mind

Chapter 1

The Future of Blockchain Technology and Cryptocurrency

-Poem

In the future of currency, we'll all be using crypto with glee,

No more coins or bills to fuss, just digital wallets to trust.

Our bank accounts will be so vast, with crypto gains that make us gasp,

But if we're not careful with our trades, we might end up with no funds to save.

Imagine buying a pizza slice, with Dogecoin at a great price,

Or trading your Bitcoin stash, for a Lamborghini that's oh-so flash.

But let's not forget the risks involved, with hackers and scams that can't be solved,

So we'll need to stay up to date, on the latest ways to secure our crypto fate.

The future of crypto is bright, but it's important to do things right,

So invest wisely and hold on tight, to a future that's sure to take flight.

Blockchain technology and cryptocurrency have come a long way since the creation of Bitcoin in 2009. As the technology evolved, so too has its potential for disrupting traditional industries and creating new opportunities for innovation.

In this section, we discussed some of the trends and predictions for the future of blockchain technology and cryptocurrency.

One trend that is expected to continue is the adoption of blockchain technology by traditional financial institutions. Many banks and financial institutions have already begun exploring the use of blockchain for streamlining processes such as cross-border payments and trade finance. This trend is likely to continue as more institutions recognize the potential benefits of blockchain technology for reducing costs and increasing efficiency.

Another trend is the continued development of decentralized finance (DeFi) applications. DeFi refers to financial applications built on blockchain technology that operate without the need for intermediaries such as banks or financial institutions. DeFi has the potential to disrupt traditional financial systems by offering new forms of lending, borrowing, and trading that are more transparent and accessible.

In terms of cryptocurrency, there is likely to be continued growth in the market as more people recognize the potential of digital assets as a store of value and means of exchange. However, as the market grows, there is also likely to be increased regulation from governments and financial institutions. This regulation may be necessary to protect consumers and prevent fraudulent activities, but it may also stifle innovation and limit the potential of blockchain technology and cryptocurrency.

Overall, the future of blockchain technology and cryptocurrency is bright, with many exciting opportunities for innovation and disruption. However, as with any emerging technology, there are also risks and uncertainties. It is important for investors and stakeholders to carefully consider the potential benefits and drawbacks of blockchain technology and cryptocurrency, and to stay informed about the latest trends and developments in the field.

Chapter 2 (Supplemental)

Tips to Keep In Mind

-Poem

Crypto, oh crypto, the risks are so great,
One wrong move and you'll be left to fate.

With scams and frauds lurking around the bend,
Your investment dreams might come to an end.

Phishing attacks are a common sight,
So watch out for those emails that may bite.

Don't click on links that seem too good,
Or you might end up in the digital hood.

And if you're not careful with your keys,
You might lose your crypto with ease.

Forget your password, or lose your phone,

And your crypto funds will be forever gone.

Then there's the market, oh so volatile,

It can be quite the financial trial.

One day it's up, and the next it's down,

Leaving you with a big crypto frown.

But despite the risks, we still invest,

In hopes of making our wallets the best.

So let's stay alert and stay informed,

And our crypto investments won't be harmed.

Take the time to learn and understand,

And you'll be on top of the crypto land.

With profits that will make you smile,

And a crypto portfolio that's worth your while.

Building wealth in cryptocurrency can be a risky endeavor, but if done correctly, it can also be very rewarding. Here are some tips to keep in mind:

1. Do your own research: Before investing in any cryptocurrency, it's important to do your due diligence and research the project thoroughly. Look into the team behind the project, the technology, and the potential use cases. This will help you make informed investment decisions.

2. Diversify your portfolio: Just like with traditional investments, it's important to diversify your cryptocurrency portfolio. Don't put all your eggs in one basket instead, consider investing in a variety of projects to spread out your risk.

3. Take a long-term approach: Cryptocurrencies can be volatile in the short term, but over the long term, they have shown impressive returns. If you're looking to build wealth in cryptocurrency, consider taking a long-term approach and holding onto your investments for several years.

4. Use dollar-cost averaging: Instead of investing a lump sum all at once, consider using dollar-cost averaging. This involves investing a fixed amount of money at regular intervals, which can help smooth out the impact of market volatility.

5. Stay informed: The cryptocurrency market is constantly changing, so it's important to stay informed about the latest developments. Follow news outlets, social media, and industry experts to stay up-to-date on the latest trends and developments in the crypto world.

Remember, building wealth in cryptocurrency is not a guaranteed endeavor, and it's important to invest only what you can afford to lose. Always exercise caution and make informed investment decisions.

I hope you did learn a thing or two from reading this book. I'll now leave you with a final poem, titled: Adventures on the Blockchain.

-Poem: Adventures on the Blockchain.

In the land of digital gold,

Where transactions are bought and sold.

There lived a little coin one day,

Who wanted to go out and play.

"I'm tired of sitting in a wallet,
I want to go out and do something, dammit!"

So it hopped onto the blockchain train,
Ready to take on the transaction lane.

The journey started out quite slow,
The blocks were big and the lines did grow.

But our little coin was determined to succeed,
So it held on tight and picked up speed.

The miners worked hard to validate,
Each and every transaction on this digital slate.

And though it seemed like an endless climb,
Our little coin was having a good time.

It bounced from block to block with glee,
A happy little coin, carefree.

It laughed and played with every hash,
And sometimes even made a little cash.

The journey was long, but oh-so fun,
Our little coin had finally begun.

To see the world beyond the wallet's hold,
And experience the blockchain's story told.

And when it finally reached its destination,
The little coin let out a proclamation.

"I may be small but I've seen it all,
And on this blockchain, I had a ball!"

So if you ever find yourself on this digital train,
Remember to enjoy the journey, don't complain.

For every transaction is a little adventure,
And every coin has a story to treasure.

Best of luck on your crypto journey!

Reference

1. Raja Santhi A, Muthuswamy P. Influence of Blockchain Technology in Manufacturing Supply Chain and Logistics. *Logistics*. 2022; 6(1):15. https://doi.org/10.3390/logistics6010015